The Last Days of
BRITISH SAINT AUGUSTINE,
1784–1785

A Spanish Census of the English Colony of East Florida

By
Lawrence H. Feldman

CLEARFIELD

Copyright © 1998
by Lawrence H. Feldman
All Rights Reserved.

Printed for
Clearfield Company, Inc. by
Genealogical Publishing Co., Inc.
Baltimore, Maryland
1998

Reprinted for
Clearfield Company, Inc. by
Genealogical Publishing Co., Inc.
Baltimore, Maryland
2003

International Standard Book Number: 0-8063-4792-9

Made in the United States of America

Table of Contents

The Census and Associated Documents iv
The East Florida Papers ix
A List of all English residents at the change of Flag in 1784 1
Appendix 1. Militia on the 6th of August 1784 81
Appendix 2. Residents on a Street and Two Islands 82
Appendix 3. Other Names mentioned in associated documents 83
Appendix 4. October 1784 Census 84
Appendix 5. "Blacks found without an owner" 87
Appendix 6. Government in British East Florida 90
References Cited 91
Index of Personal Names 93
Index of Origins 108
Index of Occupations 111
Index of Other Subjects 115

The Census and Associated Documents

In 1763 East Florida was ceded to Britain by the Treaty of Paris. The colony was returned, as a result of the treaties that ended the American War of Independence, to Spain in 1783. The manuscripts copied here represent some of the first acts of the incoming Spanish administration, a survey and census of the inhabitants of San Augustine and its dependent territories in East Florida.[1]

Most of our data comes from a manuscript, identified in associated twentieth-century papers as "A List of all English residents at the time of change of Flag," that served as a checklist of the inhabitants of the former British colony.[2] The much-handled document, with its worn and torn initial pages, dates from after the arrival of the Spanish governor. According to the East Florida Papers the Spanish governor, Zespedes, officially announced his presence and the assumption of his duties on the 13th of July, 1784 (card catalogue of the East Florida Papers at the Library of Congress). On August 14th of 1784, Brigadier General Archibald MacArthur and his staff sailed for Nassau in the Bahamas Islands (Tanner 1989:54), an event implied by the wording of entry #476 as something that had already taken place.

A second, much more limited census was prepared on the 20th of October of the same year (Appendix 4). Therefore one can assume that the "List of all English residents..." dates from between August and October of 1784. Because of the many who would soon leave, indeed who are checked off on the document as intending to leave, I

---

[1]Named locations extend from Matanzas, south of Saint Augustine, to the Georgia border. Most are either on the coast and/or close to a river.

[2]Although a census, in the sense of a systematic listing of the individuals in East Florida, it is different from most Spanish censuses of this period by not rigidly adhering to a preconceived format. It includes a petition from an individual seeking pardon from the Spanish crown, information on domestic squabbles, and other extraneous material. In this regard the census of Appendix 4, although more limited in content, is much more typical.

would assume that the document was begun in August 1784 and continuously annotated to at least October of that same year.

Because this is a genealogical research aid and not a historical study of the document, not all parts of the document were copied. Most households give a street location and/or placement in the East Florida colony. Except insofar as these data mention the names of individuals (*i.e.*, renting the house from a named person or located so many houses distant from the house of another named individual) or are noted in the sample given in Appendix 2, these data have been omitted from the present work. The same procedure applies to slave data. No slaves are mentioned unless there is a reference to a named owner or a named associated person or the slave has a last name (Appendix 5). However, most households have black slaves, and the numbers are given in the document. Black slave information provided here is thus very incomplete, and the interested reader will want to return to the document for further data on this subject.

"A List of all English residents..." is not unknown in the published literature and was used by Rasico (1990), who has published the Minorcan households given in the listing. However, this work has two advantages that previous works lacked.

(1) The author was able to work with the original at the Library of Congress rather than with the microfilm available to most researchers. The original document, which was laminated and placed in a bound volume many years ago, is for the most part in good condition and easy to read. The microfilm, which is of low quality, is difficult to read. Also, the microfilm is deficient for it appears to lack pages that may be seen in the original.[3]

(2) This is the first attempt to publish a comprehensive listing of all the entries for the white population.

---

[3]There are actually two volumes; the data in the second volume (which deals with the period after 1785), were published by Mills (1992), who worked from a microfilm copy. Some of the same households appear in both volumes, and I have noted these in the text. I did not make any effort to study the documents in the second volume.

There are some obvious problems with this document. A comprehensive listing of the indicated portions of the document is provided, but the document is not comprehensive of the entire population. Clearly, when individuals who are named as living in East Florida (*e.g.*, references to their houses) lack their own separate entry, the document has deficiencies. Perhaps some of this is due to a reluctance of the census taker to query higher officials. Thus the households of both the departing British governor (Lieutenant Colonel Patrick Tonyn) and incoming Spanish governor (Vizente Manuel de Zespedes) are missing from the household listings.

Part of the problem may reside in the chaos that the colony endured during the last years of English administration. In 1783 "over seventy-five hundred refugees reached East Florida [from Savannah and Charleston], inflating the total population to more than seventeen thousand. Yeats noted in September, 1782, that 'thousands of Refugees and Negroes arrived here from Georgia upon the evacuation of that province'" (Griffin 1983:119).

While some of these individuals were noted in "List of all English residents," many, perhaps even most, escaped notice. This was also true of the list of the British Militia on the 6th of August, 1784 (Appendix 1). Most of the militia apparently were not considered heads, or members, of established households. The "List of all English residents" was, primarily, for households already present in the colony and not for temporary residents (or soldiers) on their way to somewhere else.

These long-term (and all other) residents had eighteen months to decide if they would swear allegiance to the Spanish crown and adopt the Catholic religion or go elsewhere. During that interval, the colony kept its two sets of colonial administrators (British and Spanish) while the British settled their affairs and arranged to depart. Not all residents were willing or able to depart within these limits. Appendix 3 contains names abstracted from associated documents; many of these people were seeking an extension of time in order to sell their property.

Who were the inhabitants of British Saint Augustine? As to be expected, the vast majority were farmers (the text uses the term *labrador*). However, a surprisingly large number has some association with the sea. Seamen, fishermen, owners of schooners or other boats (even a canoe is mentioned), ship's carpenters, sailing masters, and a teacher of navigation are in the sample. Beyond this group are day laborers, plantation owners, craftsmen of all types, tanners, butchers, school teachers, bakers, and people with varied additional skills and handicrafts. British Saint Augustine was not a backwoods pioneer settlement with just one industry and one or two necessary skills.

The people were also cosmopolitan in their origins (Table 1). As to be expected, the British Isles—England, Scotland, and Ireland— are well represented as are most of the thirteen colonies of the original United States, with the Carolinas being an especially important source of people. Almost every country in Europe is represented: France, Spain, Portugal, Sweden, Switzerland, Malta, Italy, Corsica, and Translyvania (today part of Romania) as well as Greeks from various lands and even a "Jew" from Poland.

Former residents of Minorca, who had come via the failed settlement of New Smyrna (near the Mukoso inlet), formed an entire section of Saint Augustine (see Quinn 1975, Griffin 1990, and Rasico 1990 for books on the history of these Minorcans). Except for the Minorcans, most of the other groups would leave with the British; the result was a more uniform, and less interesting, colony to be ruled by the incoming Spanish administration.

Table 1. Origins of 740 entries[4]

America: 295 = 40%
South Carolina: 77 = 10%
Virginia: 66 = 9%
North Carolina: 47 = 6%
Pennsylvania: 42 = 6%
Georgia: 26 = 4%
Maryland: 9
New York: 8
Florida: 5
American: 4
Boston: 3
Nova Scotia: 2
[11][New] Jersey: 2
New England: 1
Bermuda: 1
Providence (Bahamas): 1
Carolina: 1

Europe: 404 = 55%
Scotland: 95 = 13%
[5]Balearic Islands: 91 = 12%
England: 84 = 11%
Ireland: 61 = 8%
Germany: 17
[6]Italy: 17
Corsica: 10
[7]France: 9
[8]Spain: 5
[9]Greece: 5
[10]Switzerland: 4
Poland: 2
Sweden: 1
Malta: 1
Portugal: 1
Transylvania: 1

Asia: 1 (Turkey)

None or unknown: 41 = 5%

---

[4]Based on "A List of all English residents" and Appendix 1.

[5]"Minorca" (86), "Mahon" (3), and "Mallorca" (2).

[6]Modena (1), Florence (1), Tuscany (7), Leghorn (1), Napoles (2), Venice (2), and "Italy" (3).

[7]"France" (5), Alsace (2), Brest (1), and Gascony (1).

[8]Andalucia (1), Barcelona (1), Infantes (1), Tarragona (1), and Sitges (1).

[9]The "Nation of the Greeks" (1), Crete (1), island of Milo (1), and "Morea" translated here as the Peloponnesus (1). The Smyrna reference is also included here since that individual appears in a "Petition of the Italians and Greeks" and the population of that city is known to have included many Greeks.

[10]"Switzerland" (1), Geneva (1), "Peze" [Basel?] (1), and Bern (1).

[11]The text says "Jersey." The state is closer than the English channel island.

The East Florida Papers

The papers discussed here form only one volume of a two-volume collection of census documents. The other volume has censuses from 1786 through 1814. These have been published, based upon transcription from the microfilm, by Mills (1992). These census documents of the second Spanish period provide the names of family members (including maiden names of wives) and their ages. Since there is some overlap between settlers in the British period and the subsequent era, these records can be very useful in learning more about some of the households of 1784. A third set of census-like documents, the oaths of allegiance, extend in time from 1790 to 1821. These last documents, on microfilm reel 163/164, have yet to be made available in a published form.

The East Florida Papers at the Library of Congress fill 156 linear feet of shelf space. Many of these items have never been looked at by a historian or by any researcher. The inventory often describes only large groupings without getting into detail on particular manuscripts. Hence future work with this collection could yield more census or census-like documents. Of special relevance for interpreting the documents reported on here is the manuscript bundle 208M16 (container 255, microfilm reel 89), which consists of "correspondence with British Authorities, 1784–1788." This bundle fortunately has index cards reporting on individual documents, and I footnoted appropriate references from these cards in the text.

It is due only to the tardiness of Spanish officials that researchers are not required to examine these East Florida Papers in Havana, Cuba, or Seville, Spain. In 1821 the Spanish colony of Florida was ceded to the United States. "In October 1821, several months after the formal transfer of East Florida to the United States, the records of the former Spanish government at St. Augustine were seized to prevent their being spirited to Cuba. They were organized into numbered bundles or legajos...and were made available to both American National and Florida territorial governments and to the authorities appointed to adjudicate land claims. In 1849 the records were placed under the control of the Florida Surveyor-General of the

General Land Office, Department of the Interior, where they remained (with an interruption during the Civil War) until 1905" (notes on provenance and organization from the register papers of the Library of Congress).

Hill (1916:xxiii) notes: "This archive was placed in charge of the United States Land Office and suffered many years of neglect. Finally in 1905 these papers were discovered by the Librarian of Congress, and arrangements were made to have them deposited in the Library of Congress, where they are now to be found." A Report of the Librarian of Congress for 1905, cited on the same page in Hill, adds: "The papers number 62,224 pieces, with some volumes bound under the Spanish rule. The number of papers in the volumes can hardly be determined as they are now, as the *polilla* busily bored through and through an entire volume, and even the parchment covers, until a sheet looks like a bit of lace work...."

Fortunately, the census manuscripts of 1784 do not suffer from this affliction. Aside from possible missing pages and a few damaged ones, they are in excellent condition. With the exception of certain misspellings caused by transcription in a language alien to the eighteenth-century author, they remain easy to read and available for further study and research by the interested investigator.[12]

I would like to thank the staff of the Library of Congress Manuscript Reading Room who allowed the original manuscript to be studied, intermittently, over a period of two years. I would also like to express my hope that this contribution will be useful for those seeking to learn more about the people of the last days of the British colony of East Florida.

September 5, 1997

Lawrence H. Feldman
Post Office Box 2493
Wheaton, Maryland 20915-2493
Lawrenc846@aol.com

---

[12]Inserted, in italics, in the English text are those Spanish words with uncertain, unusual, dubious, or (in a few instances) untranslatable meanings.

A List of all English residents at the change of Flag in 1784.

The document names heads of family, place of origin and number in each family. Often one finds annotations on the expected fate of these individuals. When appropriate, this listing also incorporates data from documents used for appendices 1, 3, 4 and 5. Data so incorporated is not duplicated in these appendices.

1. Cunningham, Guillermo. Page 1. Origin: Origin: Virginia.. Family Status: single. Other: William Cunningham in a statement of five Americans who are disturbing the peace of the country of 15th of July of 1784, wishes to avail himself of Spanish protection and settle in Louisiana. He is unmarried, and has seven slaves and four horses (Lockey 1949:236).

2. Mangum, Guillermo (1784 alternative spelling Mangun). Page 1. Occupation: hunter in 1783, planter in 1784. Origin: Origin: Virginia.. Family Status: wife and children. Other: William Mangum in a statement of five Americans who are disturbing the peace of the country of 15th of July 1784, wishes to avail himself of Spanish protection and settle in Louisiana. He has a wife, two children, four slaves and five horses (Lockey 1949:236).

3. [Linder, John, Senior] (surname missing in the text). Page 1. Origin: Canton of "Peze" [Basel] in Switzerland. Family Status: wife and son. Other: Given in the October 1784 census as being Juan ("the old") Linder, a surveyor who originally was from Germany with a family composed of 3 individuals who intended to move to Louisiana. He is also noted as John Linder Senior in a statement of five Americans who are disturbing the peace of the country of 15th of July 1784. The statement notes that he wishes to avail himself of Spanish protection and settle in Louisiana. And that he is a native of Basel Switzerland, has a wife, a son, twenty-two slaves and two horses (Lockey 1949:236).

4. Blyk, Juan. Page 2. Origin: Scotland. Family Status: Widower y daughter.

5. Neeley, Christobal. Page 2. Occupation: planter in 1784. Origin: Virginia. Family Status: 4 member family. Other: In 1784 intends to remain in East Florida.

6. Neeley, Roberto. Page 2. Occupation: farmer. Origin: Virginia.. Family Status: single. Other: In 1784 intends to remain in East Florida. Lives next to the river in a locality called "Newcastle."

7. Vass, Lachlam. Page 2. Origin: Scotland.

8. Young, Alexandro. Page 2. Occupation: Indian trader in the company of the English interpreter Langley Briant. Origin: North Carolina. Other: intends to stay in East Florida. Family Status: single.

9. Burchani, Josef [Burcham]. Page 3. Occupation: farmer. Origin: American. 5 member family. Servant boy called Robin King.[13] Other: in 1784 intends to move to Louisiana. As Joseph Burcham, one of the signers of Address of the Inhabitants of the River St. John of 25th of January 1785 (Lockey 1949:471).

10. King, Robin. Page 3. white boy.

11. NAME MISSING. Page 3. Origin: Origin: Scotland. Family Status: single.

12. NAME MISSING. Page 3. Occupation: farmer and carpenter. Origin: North Carolina. Family Status: wife and 3 children.

13. Sutherland, John. Page 3. Occupation: farmer. Origin: Scotland. Family Status: single.

14. Clarke, Tomas. Page 4. Origin: South Carolina.

---

[13]As Robin King, one of the signers of Address of the Inhabitants of the River St. John of 25th of January 1785 (Lockey 1949:471).

15. MacGirit, Daniel. Page 4. Occupation: farmer. Origin: South Carolina. Family Status: wife, 2 children and 2 nephews. Other: in 1784 intends to move to Louisiana. His house lot was bought from Captain Butler. As Daniel McGirth, he was named in an Address of the Inhabitants of the River St. John of 25th of January 1785 as an arrested leader of robbers and murderers (Lockey 1949:471). In January 1786 he, and his entire family, was deported to the Bahamas (Tanner 1989).

16. Brown, Gualtero. Page 5. Occupation: planter. Origin: Scotland. Family Status: single. Other: In 1784 intends to remain in East Florida.

17. Fergtet, Adam. Page 5. Occupation: carpenter but currently the foreman of Graham[14], the former governor of this province. Origin: South Carolina. Family Status: widower and 2 children.

18. Stafford, Thomas. Page 5. Occupation: carpenter. Origin: England. Family Status: single. Other: "He lives on the said Rio San Juan, 60 miles from the mouth, on the planting of Lord Hawke with the foreman." He is master of two boats.

19. Hambly, Juan. Page 6. Occupation: Indian trader. Origin: England. Family Status: wife and 3 children. Other: dependent of the House of Panton and Leslie. In 1787 listed as Anglican (Mills 1992). He was still associated with Panton and Leslie in 1804. In 1826 there is a reference to him serving as an interpreter. His wife was Indian and he may have moved afterwards to what eventually became Oklahoma (Coker and Watson 1986:325).

20. Murphy, Guillermo. Page 6. Occupation: farmer and carpenter. Origin: Pennsylvania. Family Status: wife and 3 children.

21. NAME MISSING. Page 6. Occupation: farmer. Origin: Scotland. Other: owns 500 acres of indigo ("*tina*", probably *tinta* is meant).

---

[14]Perhaps Colonel James Grant, who was one of the governors of British East Florida (see Appendix 6), is meant here.

22. Palmer, Martin. Page 6. Occupation: farmer. Origin: South Carolina. Family Status: wife and 3 children.

23. Tannyng, Juan. Page 6. Occupation: farmer. Origin: Virginia. Family Status: wife and 2 children

24. Bollison, Francisco. Page 7. Origin: Origin: North Carolina. Other: alternative spelling is Rollison.

25. Coulson, Thomas. Page 7. Occupation: farmer. Origin: South Carolina. Family Status: 2 member family. Other: In 1784 intends to remain in East Florida.

26. Lambert, Jacobo Page 7. Occupation: shoemaker and tanner. Origin: [New] Jersey. Family Status: wife. Other: His "house [is] 1 mile from Langley Briant."

27. Linsay, Page. Page 7. Origin: Scotland. Family Status: wife and son.

28. Rollins, Benjamin. Page 7. Occupation: farmer. Origin: South Carolina. Family Status: 3 children. Other: "He lives 3 miles from the house of Langley Briant, the Indian Interpreter." In 1784 he intended to remain in East Florida.

29. Rollison, Francisco. Page 7. Origin: Origin: North Carolina. Family Status: wife missing.

30. Ashworth, Josef. Page 8. Occupation: farmer. Origin: Virginia. Family Status: single. Other: As Joseph Ashworth, signed the Address of the Inhabitants of the River St. John of 25th of January 1785 (Lockey 1949:471).

31. Hall, Carlos. Page 8. Occupation: farmer. Origin: North Carolina. Family Status: wife. Other: in 1784 intends to stay in East Florida. As Charles Hall, is one of the signers of Address of the Inhabitants of the River St. John of 25th of January 1785 (Lockey 1949:471).

32. Mott, Hanah. Page 8. Origin: South Carolina.

33. NAME MISSING. Page 8. Origin: Georgia.

34. White, Jacobo. Page 8. Occupation: tailor. Origin: Virginia. Family Status: 2 brothers and 1 sister.

35. Forbes, Jacobo. Page 9. Occupation: shoemaker and farmer. Origin: Bermuda ["Bermeja"]. Family Status: single. Other: "lives with an old widow called Isabel Macdon..".

36. NAME MISSING. Page 9. Occupation: farmer. Origin: Ireland.

37. Waldron, Luisa. Page 9. Occupation: bartender and gardener. Origin: Ireland. Family Status: widow. Other: Lyfford Waldron was one of the signers of an "Address of the Principal Inhabitants to Governor Tonyn" of June 6, 1783 (Lockey 1949:114). In 1784 Luisa Waldron intends to remain in East Florida. She "has ten acres of land next to the old Spanish stockade two leagues from the city. She has in Apalache 10 slaves belonging to her dead husband and a sister who is well married in Havana." Griffin (1983:126-127) notes that for a time during 1784/85 she was accused of harboring a runaway slave. She was placed in confinement, her horse was confiscated and house ransacked by Spanish soldiers. According to Tanner (1989:51), also known as Mrs. Welsh and Mrs. Proctor.

38, Ansel, Martin. Page 10. Occupation: ship's carpenter. Origin: South Carolina. Other: "He lives in the house of Don Juan Hopkins." and "is finishing the construction of a schooner in the Rio San Juan."

39. Batingoy, Jacobo. Page 10. Occupation: carpenter. Origin: Maryland. Family Status: wife and 5 children. Other: in 1784 he intends to stay in East Florida.

40. Clarke. Page 10. Occupation: farmer. Origin: Scotland. Family Status: widower.

41. Pritchard, Eduardo. Page 10. Occupation: farmer. Origin: Pennsylvania. Family Status: single. Other: "He lives at the ranch of Mr. Graystock.[15]"

42. Thompson. Page 10. Occupation: farmer. Origin: Pennsylvania.

43. Harrison. Page 11. Occupation: farmer. Origin: Virginia. Family Status: wife. Brother of Samuel Harrison.

44. Harrison, Samuel. Page 11. Occupation: farmer. Origin: Virginia. Family Status: wife and son.

45. Oria, Arturo. Page 11. Occupation: farmer. Origin: Georgia. Family Status: single. Other: "lives with previously cited Willis Pace."

46. Pace, Willis. Page 11. Origin: North Carolina. Family Status: single.

47. Sanfort, Jacobo. Page 11. carpenter. Origin: Virginia. Family Status: wife and son. Other: has his own schooner.

48. Davis, Guillermo. Page 12. Origin: Virginia. Family Status: wife, son and orphan.

49. Ladson, Juan. Page 12. Occupation: farmer. Origin: South Carolina. Family Status: wife. Other: in 1784 intends to stay in East Florida. As John C. Ladson, signed the Address of the Inhabitants of the River St. John of 25th of January 1785 (Lockey 1949:471). In 1787 listed as Juan Conway Ladson (Mills 1992).

50. Stout, Jose. Page 12. Occupation: farmer. Origin: Transylvania " of the Emperor" [today part of Romania]. Family Status: wife and 4 children.

51. Swiney, Maria. Page 12. Occupation: farmer. Origin: South Carolina. Family Status: widow. Other: She owns Mount Tucker ranch.

---

[15]As William Graystock, one of the signers of Address of the Inhabitants of the River St. John of 25th of January 1785 (Lockey 1949:471).

52. Towin, Roberto. Page 12. Origin: North Carolina. Family Status: wife. Other: He has a white boy called Ricardo Colman. He lived by "the site called Mount Pleasant."

53. Williams, Enrique. Page 12. Occupation: farmer. Origin: North Carolina. Family Status: wife and 8 children.

54. Hodge, David. Page 13. Occupation: supervisor on the plantation of Mr. Pevit. Origin: Virginia. Family Status: wife.

55. Houston, Juan. Page 13. Occupation: in 1873- maker of small boats and canoes; in 1784- carpenter. Origin: Georgia. Family Status: wife and 2 children. Other: in 1784 intends to remain in East Florida. Other: Given in 1787 as farmer (Mills 1992).

56. Humphrys, David. Page 13. Occupation: farmer. Origin: South Carolina. Family Status: single.

57. Humphrys, Juan. Page 13. Occupation: farmer. Origin: Pennsylvania.

58. Kane, Guillermo. Page 13. Occupation: farmer. Origin: Pennsylvania. Family Status: wife and 4 children. Other: in 1784 intends to remain in East Florida. In 1787 is Guillermo Kean (Mills 1992).

59. NAME MISSING. Page 13. Occupation: farmer. Origin: Ireland. Family Status: wife and a son.

60. NAME MISSING. Page 13. Origin: Scotland. Family Status: wife and a son. Other: Has eight married children in the province.

61. Bean, Juan. Page 14. Origin: Sweden. Family Status: wife.

62. Burnett, Juan. Page 14. Occupation: farmer. Origin: New York. Family Status: wife and 8 children. Other: As John Burnett, signed the Address of the Inhabitants of the River St. John (Lockey 1949:471). He lived near Mount Pleasant.

63. Ferguson, Juan. Page 14. Other: See entry #66.

64. Fenner, Jose. Page 14. Occupation: farmer. Origin: Virginia. Family Status: wife. Other: As Joseph Fenner, is one of the signers of Address of the Inhabitants of the River St. John of 25th of January 1785 (Lockey 1949:471).

65. Hughes, Jose. Page 14. Occupation: mason. Origin: England. Family Status: widower and son. Other: in 1787 as bricklayer and farmer (Mills 1992).

66. Laird, Jacobo. Page 14. Occupation: farmer. Origin: Pennsylvania. Family Status: single. Other: lives with a free mulato called Juan Ferguson.

67. Rols, Juan. Page 14. Origin: Scotland.

68. Egan, Esteban. Page 15. Occupation: planter and farmer. Origin: Ireland. Family Status: wife and 3 children. Other: Stevan Egan, "agent for the Estate of the Right Honorable the late Earl of Egmont and himself," signed the Address of the British Subjects, dated on the 15th of February of 1785, seeking a prolongation of the stipulated term of residence. (Lockey 1949: 521-522). As Stephen Egan, signed the Address thanking Governor Zespedes "with the warmest acknowledgement and thanks for security and tranquility afforded us ... during the whole course of the Evacuation," dated 24th of March 1785 (Lockey 1949: 532-533).

69. Fatio, Don Francisco Felipe. Page 15. Occupation: planter in 1784. Origin: Berne Switzerland. Family Status: wife and 2 children, in 1784 there are 7 in his family. Other: Griffin (1983: 132) notes "he remained to oversee his extensive plantation holdings on the St. Johns River. He had an Italian wife, and as a gentleman and a scholar, spoke six languages. Much of his time was spent in his house in town, and like Leslie, he was often called into service as a lay judge to settle claims such as that of Louisa Waldron." As Francis P. Fatio, he signed the Address from the

British Subjects thanking Governor Zespedes "with the warmest acknowledgment and thanks for security and tranquillity afforded ... during the ... Evacuation," dated 24th of March 1785 (Lockey 1949: 532-533). In 1787 his ranch was farmed by his son (Mills 1992). As Lewis Fatio he signed the "Address of the Principal Inhabitants to Governor Tonyn" of June 6, 1783 (Lockey 1949:115).

70. Martin, Don Juan. Page 15. Origin: Scotland. Family Status: wife and son. As John Martin, is one of the signers of an "Address of the Principal Inhabitants to Governor Tonyn" of June 6, 1783 (Lockey 1949:115).

71. Robinson, Don Jose. Page 15. Occupation: "Had been Colonel," planter in 1784. Origin: Virginia. Family Status: wife and 3 children. Other: "Lieutenant Colonel of a battalion of militia of 300 men organized after the war." In 1784 intended to remain in East Florida. As Joseph Robinson, he signed the Address thanking Governor Zespedes "with the warmest acknowledgment and thanks for security and tranquillity afforded ... during the ... Evacuation," dated 24th of March 1785 (Lockey 1949: 532-533).

72. Rogue, Don Santiago de la. Page 15. Occupation: physician. Origin: Gascony France. Family Status: single. Other: Assisted the Spanish army in the taking of Mobile and Pensacola.

73. Turnbull, Michel ? [in October "Don Choll" Turnbull]. Page 15. Occupation: "gentleman" planter. Origin: Smyrna [today Izmir Turkey]. Family Status: single. Other: in 1784 intends to remain in East Florida. Religion is Catholic. He is the son of English parents.[16]

74. Wood, Don Juan. Page 15. Origin: Scotland. Other: As John Wood, is one of the signers of an "Address of the Principal Inhabitants to Governor Tonyn" of June 6, 1783 (Lockey 1949:115).

75. Boak, Don Thomas. Page 16. Origin: England. Family Status: single.

---

[16]One wonders what connection, if any, this individual has with Dr. Andrew Turnbull who established the settlement of New Smyrna, and married a lady born in the Smyrna of Asia Minor.

76. Edwards, Don Pedro. Page 16. Occupation: private secretary of the former governor. Origin: England. Family Status: wife and 3 children. Other: As Peter Edwards, he is one of the signers of an "Address of the Principal Inhabitants to Governor Tonyn" of June 6, 1783 (Lockey 1949:115).

77. Flemming, Don Jorje. Page 16. Origin: Ireland. Family Status: single. Other: As George Flyming Oneal, signed Address from the British Subjects thanking Governor Zespedes "with the warmest acknowledgment and thanks for security and tranquillity afforded us ... during the whole course of the Evacuation," dated 24th of March 1785 (Lockey 1949: 532-533).

78. Oneill, Don Jacobo. Page 16. Occupation: businessman. Origin: Ireland. Family Status: wife and 5 children.

79. Orr, Don Thomas. Page 16. Occupation: businessman. Origin: Scotland. Family Status: single. Other: Thomas Orr is one of the signers of a "Memorial and Petition of the Inhabitants of East Florida" of September 11, 1783 (Lockey 1949:158). Thomas Orr is one of the signers of an Address of the British Subjects, dated on the 15th of February of 1785, seeking a prolongation of the stipulated term of residence. (Lockey 1949:521-522). As Thomas Orr signed Address from the British Subjects thanking Governor Zespedes "with the warmest acknowledgment and thanks for security and tranquillity afforded us ... during the whole course of the Evacuation," dated 24th of March 1785 (Lockey 1949: 532-533).

80. Amoss, Adan. Page 17. Occupation: businessman. Origin: Scotland. Family Status: single. Other: "He lives in a house in front of that of Don Jacobo [Oneill]." He is a partner in the business of Jacobo Oneill. Adam Amoss is one of the signers of an "Address of the Principal Inhabitants to Governor Tonyn" of June 6, 1783 (Lockey 1949:115).

81. MacKinnon, Don Guillermo. Page 17. Occupation: executor of the will [*albareda* in text = *albecea* ?] of the late colonel Stewart; in 1784 a planter. Origin: Scotland. Family Status: wife and 2 children. Other: William MacKinnon is one of the signers of an Address of the British Subjects, dated on the 15th of February of 1785, seeking a prolongation of the stipulated term of residence. (Lockey 1949:521-522). He lived "4 miles from the city at the site called Oak Forest."

82. Spalding, Don Jacobo. Page 17. Occupation: was a businessman but now a farmer. Origin: Scotland. Family Status: wife and son.

83. Tumio [or Tunno], Don Tomas. Page 17. Occupation: businessman. Origin: Scotland. Family Status: single. Other: Juan Reynolds and Juan Mackenzie hold the power of attorney for the sale of his property. As John Tunno, he is one of the signers of "Address of the Principal Inhabitants to Governor Tonyn" of June 6, 1783 (Lockey 1949:115). As Thomas Tunno, he is one of the signers of an Address of the British Subjects, dated on the 15th of February of 1785, seeking a prolongation of the stipulated term of residence; and also one of the signers of the Address, dated 24th of March 1785, from the British Subjects thanking Governor Zespedes "with the warmest acknowledgment and thanks for security and tranquillity afforded us ... during the whole course of the Evacuation," (Lockey 1949: 521-522, 532-533).

84. MacKenzie, Don Juan. Page 18. Occupation: businessman. Family Status: single. Other: John McKenzie is one of the signers of an Address of the British Subjects, dated on the 15th of February of 1785, seeking a prolongation of the stipulated term of residence. (Lockey 1949:521-522). As J. McKenzie signed Address from the British Subjects thanking Governor Zespedes "with the warmest acknowledgment and thanks for security and tranquillity afforded us ... during the whole course of the Evacuation," dated 24th of March 1785 (Lockey 1949: 532-533).

85. Pevit, Don Jose. Page 18. Occupation: planter. Origin: England. Family Status: wife. Other: had been major of the militia and a

member of the lower house of the assembly (see Schafer 1983:118-119 for further details on the legislature). In 1784 he intends to stay in East Florida. As Joseph Peavett, he signed an "Address" thanking Governor Zespedes "with the warmest acknowledgement and thanks for security and tranquility afforded us ... during ... the Evacuation," dated 24th of March 1785 (Lockey 1949: 532-533).

86. Sheriff, Don Pedro and his companion, Juan Falconer. Page 18. Occupation: businessmen. Origin: Scotland. Family Status: both are single. Other: they rent a "warehouse for tanners." Peter Shirreff signed the "Address of the Principal Inhabitants to Governor Tonyn" of June 6, 1783 (Lockey 1949:114). John Falconer signed the "Memorial and Petition of the Inhabitants of East Florida" of September 11, 1783 (Lockey 1949:159).

87. Storr, Don Juan. Pages 18-19. Occupation: businessman. Origin: England. Family Status: wife and son. Other: John Storr signed the "Memorial and Petition of the Inhabitants of East Florida" of September 11, 1783, an "Address" of the 15th of February of 1785 seeking a prolongation of the stipulated term of residence and the Address from the British Subjects thanking Governor Zespedes "with the warmest acknowledgement and thanks for security and tranquility afforded us ... during ... the Evacuation," dated 24th of March 1785 (Lockey 1949:158, 521-522, 532-533).

88. Briant, Langley. Page 19. Occupation: interpreter and Indian trader. Origin: North Carolina. Family Status: wife and son. Other: speaks Creek and Seminole. Partner with Alexandro Young who also intends to remain in the province.

89. Moss, Don Jacobo. Page 19. Occupation: businessman. Origin: England. Family Status: single. Other: owns two schooners.

90. Duget, Don Guillermo and David Macreddy. Page 20. Occupation: businessman. Origin: Scotland. Family Status: both are single. The residence is also occupied by the English commissioner for the Evacuation [Mr.] Bron [Don Guillermo Brown, see entry # 96].

91. Johnson, Don Juan. Page 20. Occupation: businessman. Origin: Scotland. Family Status: single. Other: his companion is Juan Michel and the two boys in his household are Eduardo Mortimer and Guillermo Gueli. As John Johnson signed Address from the British Subjects thanking Governor Zespedes "with the warmest acknowledgement and thanks for security and tranquility afforded us ... during the whole course of the Evacuation," dated 24th of March 1785 (Lockey 1949: 532-533).

92. Morris, Don Juan. Page 20. Occupation: businessman. Origin: Scotland. Family Status: single. Other: John Morris is one of the signers of a "Memorial and Petition of the Inhabitants of East Florida" of September 11, 1783 (Lockey 1949:158).

93. Clarke, Dona Honoria. Pages 20-21. Occupation: planter. Origin: Ireland. Family Status: widow and 4 children. Other: in 1784 intends to remain in East Florida. In 1786, Catholic, age 40 (Mills 1992).

94. Farley, Don Samuel. Page 21. Occupation: lawyer. Origin: England. Family Status: wife and daughter. Other: "He lives in a house belonging to Francisco Sanches." Samuel Farley is one of the signers of a "Memorial and Petition of the Inhabitants of East Florida" of September 11, 1783 (Lockey 1949:158).

95. Heley, Don Juan. Page 21. Occupation: tax collector (*controlor de rentas*). Origin: England. Family Status: single.

96. Brown, Don Guillermo. Page 22. Occupation: British commissioner for the evacuation of the fort. Origin: Scotland. Family Status: wife and 2 children. Other: This may be the same William Brown who was Speaker of the Lower House of the colonial legislature from March 1781- March 1784 (Schafer 1983:118-119).

97. Holmes, Don Juan. Page 22. Occupation: Head Notary and Head of customs. Origin: South Carolina. Family Status: 3 children. Other: goes to Charleston in the schooner William Maid. John Holmes is one of the signers of an "Address of the Principal Inhabitants to

Governor Tonyn" of June 6, 1783 (Lockey 1949:115). Mowat (1964:164) identifies as Comptroller of Customs from 1779 and Deputy Collector of Customs.

98. Hume, Don Jacobo.[17] Page 22. Occupation: Former Chief Justice of the English governor. Origin: South Carolina. Family Status: household includes a lady companion of his mistress, a nephew of the same and a white servant called Juan Makoy. Other: As John James Hume, is one of the signers of an "Address of the Principal Inhabitants to Governor Tonyn" of June 6, 1783 (Lockey 1949:114).

99. Scott, Don Roberto. Page 22. Occupation: physician. Origin: England. Family Status: single. Other: "He is next to the house of Colonel Brown." Robert Scott is one of the signers of an "Address of the Principal Inhabitants to Governor Tonyn" of June 6, 1783 (Lockey 1949:115). As Robert Scott, signed Address from the British Subjects thanking Governor Zespedes "with the warmest acknowledgment and thanks for security and tranquillity afforded us ... during the whole course of the Evacuation," dated 24th of March 1785 (Lockey 1949: 532-533).

100. Capo, Lorenzo. Page 23. Occupation: sexton. Origin: Minorca. Family Status: wife and 2 children. Other: In 1786, age 40 (Mills 1992), (Mercadal, Minorca; Rasico 1990:159). Lorenzo Capo in a memorial of July 12, 1784, requests recognition as a natural-born subject (Lockey 1949:233).

101. Leonardi, Roque. Page 23. Occupation: wine trader (farmer in 1787). Origin: Modena in 1787 (Mills 1992:49) (Duchy of Guanclasen in 1784 text) Italy. Family Status: wife and 3 children. Other: "works for Don Pedro Camps." Camps, otherwise known as Father or Doctor Camps, was the parish priest of the Minorcans (Schafer 1983:118). There is a passing reference to him on page 169 of this document. Roco Leonardy, in a memorial of July 12, 1784, requests recognition as a natural-born subject (Lockey 1949:232).

---

[17]There is a letter of Jonyn, dated 14th of August 1784, in which he encloses the "opinion of the former Chief British Justice Jacobo Hume," (card index to the papers of the East Florida collection).

102. MacHenry, Guillermo. Page 23. Occupation: trader in distilled liquor and beer, carpenter. Origin: Ireland. Family Status: widower. Other: "His house is close to that of Don Jesse Fish."

103. Sanchez, Francisco. Page 23. Occupation: farmer. Origin: East Florida. Family Status: single and 7 children. Other: in 1786, planter, 40 years old (Mills 1992). Griffin (1983: 132-133) notes "Francisco Xavier Sanchez was about seventeen when the British flag was raised in 1763. He became a successful planter in the English era, skillfully withstanding Tonyn's[18] attempt to implicate him in the banditti conspiracies. By the Spanish return he had a mulatto mistress whose progeny he recognized as his legal heirs. Later he... took a young wife... and by the time of his death in 1807 was one of the most venerated citizens in town."

104. Bremarach, Pedro. Page 24. Occupation: carpenter. Origin: Corsica. Family Status: widower and 2 children.

105. Buchantine, Luis. Page 24. Occupation: sailor. Origin: Tuscany Italy. Family Status: wife. Other: left East Florida. Other: in 1786 listed as Buchentiny, farmer, Leghorn, age 39, house in the Greek neighborhood (of Saint Augustine), left (Mills 1992). As Luigi Bruciantiny, in a memorial of July 12, 1784, requests recognition as a natural-born subject (Lockey 1949:233).

106. Etienne, Sebastian. Page 24. Occupation: gardener. Origin: France. Family Status: wife and 3 children. Other: Possibly listed, in 1786, as Sebastian Esteve, jailer, age 50 (Mills 1992).

107. Granopoli, Juan. Page 24. Occupation: carpenter. Origin: Peloponnesus Greece ("Morea"). Family Status: wife. Other: probably Juan Chanopoly in 1787 (Mills 1992:43). As Juan Chanopli listed in the Petition of the Italians and Greeks of the 27th of January 1787 (Lockey 1949:463).

---

[18]Lieutenant Colonel Patrick Tonyn, the second and last permanent English governor of the colony.

108. Medici, Elias. Page 24. Origin: Corsica. Family Status: widower and 3 children. Elia Medici in a memorial of July 12, 1784, requests recognition as a natural-born subject (Lockey 1949:232).

109. Meyes, Juana Maria. Page 24. Origin: Minorca. Family Status: widow and 4 children.

110. Ortega, Sebastian. Page 24. Origin: Minorca. Family Status: wife and married children. Other: in 1786, Ortegas, age 33 (Mills 1992). As Sebastian Ortegas in a memorial of July 12, 1784, requests recognition as a natural-born subject (Lockey 1949:233).

111. Segui, Miguel. Page 24. Origin: Minorca. Family Status: wife, 4 daughters, 1 son. Other: in 1786, age 36 (Mills 1992). (Miquel Segui, Ciudadela Minorca, carpenter, fisherman; Rasico 1990: 168).

112. Ansiau, Francisco. Page 25. Occupation: farmer. Origin: Minorca. Family Status: wife and 5 children.

113. Cosifacho, Pedro. Page 25. Occupation: shopkeeper. Origin: Corsica. Family Status: wife and 5 children. Other: owns schooner. As Pietro Cozifaccy, in a memorial of July 12, 1784, requests recognition as a natural-born subject (Lockey 1949:233). In 1787 owns clothing shop (Mills 1992).

114. Martineli, Domingo. Page 25. Occupation: master of a schooner. Venice Italy. Family Status: wife and 2 children.

115. Napoles, Antonio Estevan. Page 25. Occupation: master of a schooner. Origin: Corsica. Family Status: single.

116. Ortega, Sebastian the Younger. Page 25. Occupation: stonecutter. Origin: Minorca. Family Status: wife and 3 children. (Sebastian Ortegas, Rasico 1990: 164).

117. Pelliser, Francisco. Page 25. Occupation: carpenter. Origin: Mallorca. Family Status: wife and 3 children. (Francesc Pellicer, Alayor Minorca; Rasico 1990: 164). Francisco Pelliser in a memorial

of July 12, 1784, requests recognition as a natural-born subject (Lockey 1949:233).

118. Machogui, Joaquin. Pages 25-26. Occupation: master of a schooner. Origin: Tuscany Italy. Family Status: wife and 3 children.

119. Cavedo, Juan, the Younger. Page 26. Origin: Minorca. Family Status: single. Son of the widow Ines Cavedo.

120. Chuaneda, Jose. Page 26. Occupation: sailor with brother Juan. Origin: Minorca. Other: absent.

121. Estefanople, Nicolas. Page 26. Occupation: carpenter. Origin: Corsica. Family Status: wife and 3 children. Other: "He lives on the block of Don Jese Fish." In 1786, he was 38 years old (Mills 1992).

122. Foche, Luis. Page 26. Occupation: rope maker and fisherman. Origin: Tuscany Italy. Family Status: wife. Other: "His house is near that of Don Juan Martin."

123. Jusovat, Juan. Page 26. Occupation: farmer. Origin: Mallorca. Family Status: wife and 4 children.

124. Marcos, Andres. Page 26. Occupation: master of sloop. Origin: Minorca. Family Status: wife and 3 children. (Andreu Marcos; Rasico 1990: 163).

125. Solom, Juan. Page 26. Occupation: farmer. Origin: Minorca. Family Status: wife, 2 children. Other: in 1786 age 35 (Mills 1992). As Juan Selom, in a memorial of July 12, 1784, requests recognition as a natural-born subject (Lockey 1949:233).

126. Suitas, Madalena. Page 26. Occupation: tailor. Origin: Minorca. Family Status: widow. Her son Bartolome, who is ruled by her, is a tailor.

127. Apunién, Antonio. Page 27. Occupation: sailor. Origin: Minorca. Family Status: single.

128. Cardona, Jose Hernandez. Page 27. Occupation: farmer and fisherman. Origin: Minorca. Family Status: wife and son. Other: As Josef Hernández Cardona, in a memorial of July 12, 1784, requests recognition as a natural-born subject (Lockey 1949:233).

129. Chuariedas, Juan. Page 27. Occupation: blacksmith. Origin: Minorca. Family Status: wife and son.

130. Grasias, Miguel. Page 27. Occupation: fisherman. Origin: [San Felipe] Minorca. Family Status: wife and son. Other: in 1786, as Gracias, was 30 years old (Mills 1992). (Miquel Gracies, also farmer; Rasico 1990: 162). Michel Grazies, on the 12th of July 1784, requests recognition as a natural-born subject (Lockey 1949:233).

131. Hernandez, Diego. Page 27. Occupation: farmer. Origin: Minorca. Family Status: wife and 4 children. Other: (San Felipe, Minorca; Rasico 1990:162). In a memorial of July 12, 1784, requests recognition as a natural-born subject (Lockey 1949:233).

132. Hudson, Don Juan. Page 27. Occupation: fisherman and planter. Origin: Ireland. Family Status: single. Other: in 1784 intends to remain in East Florida. In 1786, Catholic, age 28 (Mills 1992). Entry for same individual on page 53 crossed out in original document. "John Hudson, a young Irish catholic, came from Havana on the earliest boat. By 1786 he had married a rich fifty-six-year-old English widow, Mary Evans (Peavett), who owned a thriving inn on St. Francis Street across from the barracks, as well as several plantations. This May-December marriage led to disaster, for John gambled away most of Mary's fortune, and as matters grew worse was clapped into the guardhouse for... wiping his backside with one of the governor's edicts. In 1791 he was banished to live twenty miles from the city gate at their only remaining plantation, New Waterford, where he died a year later," (Griffin 1983: 133).

133. Marin, Francisco. Page 27. Occupation: shoemaker. Origin: Tarragona Spain. Family Status: wife and son. Other: in 1786, 65 years old (Mills 1992). (Francesc Marin, Rasico 1990: 163). As Francisco Marin in a memorial of July 12, 1784, requests

recognition as a natural-born subject (Lockey 1949:233).

134. Tremol, Francisco. Page 27. Occupation: fisherman. Origin: Minorca. Family Status: single. Other: He lives with brother in law Luis Soche. (Francese Tremol, Rasico 1990: 168).

135. Hernandez Victor, Jose. Page 27. Occupation: stonecutter and fisherman. Origin: Minorca. Family Status: wife and 3 children. (Josep Hernandez Victori, Rasico 1990: 162).

136. Bagueri, Ansel. Page 28. Occupation: experienced harbor pilot ([*platico* in text = *practico*] *de la barra*). Origin: Tuscany Italy. Family Status: wife and 3 daughters.

137. Capella, Lorenzo. Page 28. Occupation: fisherman. Origin: Minorca. Family Status: single. (Ciudadela Minorca, farmer, fisherman, sailor; Rasico 1990:159). Lives with unwed brother Joseph Arnau. Other: in 1787 fisherman and farmer (Mills 1992). (San Felipe, Minorca, farmer; Rasico 1990:159). As Lorenzo Capella, in a memorial of July 12, 1784, requests recognition as a natural-born subject (Lockey 1949:233).

138. Carreras, Juan. Page 28. Occupation: seller of distilled liquor. Origin: Minorca. Family Status: widower. Other: in 1786, age 40 (Mills 1992). (Joan Carreres, Mahon, Minorca, carpenter, sailor, seller of aguardiente; Rasico 1990:159). As Juan Carrera, in a memorial of July 12, 1784, requests recognition as a natural-born subject (Lockey 1949:233).

139. Clav, Jorje. Page 28. Occupation: farmer and fisherman. Origin: Minorca. Family Status: single and unmarried sister. Other: in 1786 as Jorje Clak, age 30 (Jordi Clar ?, San Felipe, Minorca; Rasico 1990: 160).

140. Girimalde, Eulalia. Page 28. Occupation: oldest son is sailor. Origin: Minorca. Family Status: widow and 3 children.

141. Lorenza, Paula. Page 28. Occupation: laundress (*collendo* and *lavando*). Origin: Minorca. Family Status: widow and 2 children.

142. Pachete, Andres. Page 28. Occupation: barber. Origin: Napoles. Family Status: wife and 4 children. Other: Andres Pasety, farmer in 1787 (Mills 1992:42). As Andrea Pacetti, in a memorial of July 12, 1784, requests recognition as a natural-born subject (Lockey 1949:233). As Andres Pazeti listed in Petition of the Italians and Greeks of the 27th of January 1787 (Lockey 1949:463).

143. Pope, Gaspar. Page 28. Occupation: farmer. Smyrna [today Izmir Turkey]. Family Status: wife. Other: in 1787 name spelt Popee (Mills 1992). As Gaspar Popi, listed in the Petition of the Italians and Greeks of the 27th of January 1787 (Lockey 1949:463).

144. Badell, Pedro. Page 29. Occupation: farmer. Origin: Minorca. Family Status: wife and 4 children.

145. Figuera, Bartolome. Page 29. Occupation: fisherman. Origin: Mahon, Minorca. Family Status: wife and 2 children. (Bartomeu Figuera, Ciudadela Minorca, Rasico 1990: 161).

146. Mabrionat, Anastario. Page 29. Occupation: farmer. Origin: island of Milos Greece. Family Status: wife and 2 children. Other: in 1787 as Antonio Mabromaty (Mills 1992). As Anastasy Mauromati in a memorial of July 12, 1784, requests recognition as a natural-born subject (Lockey 1949:233).

147. Ortega, Lazaro. Page 29. Occupation: farmer. Origin: Minorca. Family Status: wife and 1 son. Other: (Llatzer Ortegas, San Felipe, Minorca; Rasico 1990: 164). As Lazaro Ortegas, in a memorial of July 12, 1784, requests recognition as a natural-born subject (Lockey 1949:233).

148. Pons, Jose. Page 29. Occupation: baker. Origin: Mahon, Minorca. Family Status: wife and 5 children.
(Josep Pons, Ciudadela Minorca; Rasico 1990:165)

149. Tallani, Francisco. Page 29. Occupation: sailor. Origin: Tuscany Italy. Family Status: wife and 3 children.

150. Fluxa, Juan. Page 30. Occupation: farmer and fisherman. Origin: Minorca. Family Status: wife. (Joan Fluixa, Rasico 1990: 161).

151. Pedulach, Demetrio. Page 30. Occupation: fisherman and sailor. Origin: island of Crete, Greece. Family Status: wife and 3 children. Other: in 1787 name spelt Tedulache, noted that has schooner and is of the Greek church (Mills 1992).

152. Pehgrin, Matheo. Page 30. Occupation: farmer. Origin: Tuscany Italy. Family Status: wife and son. Other: As Matheo Pelegrin, listed in the Petition of the Italians and Greeks of the 27th of January 1787 (Lockey 1949:463).

153. Portell, Juan. Page 30. Occupation: shoemaker. Origin: Minorca. Family Status: wife and son. (Joan Portella, Rasico 1990: 165) As Juan Portella, in a memorial of July 12, 1784, requests recognition as a natural-born subject (Lockey 1949:233).

154. Rose, Jose. Page 30. Occupation: farmer. Origin: Florence, Italy. Family Status: wife and 4 children. Other: As Josef Ross, listed in Petition of the Italians and Greeks of the 27th of January 1787 (Lockey 1949:463).

155. Solom, Antonio. Page 30. Occupation: fisherman. Origin: Minorca. Family Status: single.

156. Triay, Pedro. Page 30. Origin: Minorca. Family Status: single. Lives with mother and uncle. (Pere Triay, Mahon, Minorca, farmer, Rasico 1990: 169).

157. Elsini, Antonio. Page 31. Occupation: farmer. Origin: Minorca. Family Status: wife and 3 children.

158. Lloufri, Bartolome. Page 31. Occupation: farmer. Origin: Minorca. Family Status: wife and son. (Bartomeu Llofriu, Alayor Minorca;, farmer and sailor, Rasico 1990: 162). As Bartolomé Llafrui, in a memorial of July 12, 1784, requests recognition as a natural-born subject (Lockey 1949:233).

159. Pons, Mathias. Page 31. Occupation: farmer. Origin: Minorca. Family Status: wife and 2 children. Other: in 1787, Mahon (Mills 1992). As Mathias Pons in a memorial of July 12, 1784, requests recognition as a natural-born subject (Lockey 1949:233).

160. Sigui, Diego. Page 31. Occupation: farmer. Origin: Minorca. Family Status: wife and son. Other: As Diego Segui in a memorial of July 12, 1784, requests recognition as a natural-born subject (Lockey 1949:233).

161. Triay, Juan. Page 31. Occupation: farmer. Origin: Minorca. Family Status: wife and 3 children. Other: in 1786, age of 32 (Mills 1992) (Joan Triay, Mahon, Minorca; Rasico 1990). As Juan Triay in a memorial of July 12, 1784, requests recognition as a natural-born subject (Lockey 1949:233).

162. Bausina, Bartholome. Page 32. Occupation: farmer. Origin: Minorca. Family Status: wife and son.

163. Caldas, Pedro de. Page 32. Occupation: fisherman. Origin: Andalucia Spain Family Status: single.

164. Puselograpo, Francisco. Page 32. Occupation: farmer. Origin: Corsica. Family Status: wife and 2 children.

165. Segui, Bernardo. Page 32. Occupation: shopkeeper and baker. Origin: Minorca. Family Status: wife and 6 children. Other: in 1786 the age is given as 44 (Mills 1992).

166. Segui, Juan. Page 32. Occupation: farmer. Origin: Minorca. Family Status: wife and son. Other: left East Florida. In 1786 age given as 30 (Mills 1992). (Joan Segui, Ciudadela Minorca, farmer and fisherman; Rasico 1990: 167). As Juan Segui, in a memorial of July 12, 1784, requests recognition as a natural-born subject (Lockey 1949:233).

167. Villalonga, Miguel. Page 32. Occupation: farmer. Origin: Minorca. Family Status: wife and 3 children. Other: in 1786, age 29 (Mills 1992). (Miquel Villalonga, Alayor Minorca; Rasico 1990: 169).

168. Capo, Juan. Page 33. Occupation: farmer. Origin: Minorca. Family Status: wife and 4 children. Other: In 1786, age is 50 (Mills 1992). (Ciudadela Minorca; Rasico 1990:159). As Juan Capo, in a memorial of July 12, 1784, requests recognition as a natural-born subject (Lockey 1949:233).

169. Chemares, Rafael. Page 33. Occupation: farmer. Origin: Minorca. Family Status: wife and 2 children. Other: alternative spelling is Ximenes. In 1786, age is 50 (Mills 1992). (Rafel Ximenes, Alayor Minorca;, farmer, stonecutter, Rasico 1990: 169).

170. Espinosa, Jose. Page 33. Occupation: fisherman. Origin: Minorca. Family Status: wife and 2 children. Other: alternative spelling for the name is Espinete. In 1786, age is age 50 (Mills 1992). Owner of a dugout canoe.

171. Fluxa, Pedro. Page 33. Occupation: farmer. Origin: Minorca. Family Status: wife. (Pere Fluixa, Rasico 1990: 161).

172. Ortega, Ignacio. Page 33. Occupation: stonecutter. Origin: Minorca. widower. (Ignaci Ortegas, San Felipe, Minorca Rasico 1990: 164).

173. Salort, Francisco. Page 33. Occupation: farmer. Origin: Minorca. Family Status: wife. (Francesc Salord, Ciudadela Minorca, Rasico 1990: 167). As Francisco Selord, in a memorial of July 12, 1784, requests recognition as a natural-born subject (Lockey 1949:233).

174. Sante, Pasqual de. Page 33. Occupation: fisherman Origin: Naples, Italy. Family Status: wife and 2 children.

175. Andres, Juan. Page 34. Occupation: farmer. Origin: Minorca. Family Status: wife and 5 children.

176. Andreu, Thomas. Page 34. Occupation: farmer. Origin: Minorca. Family Status: wife and son. Other: in 1786, age 26 (Mills 1992). Mercadal, Minorca (Rasico 1990:158).

177. Candioli, Francisco. Page 34. Occupation: sailor. Origin: Venice Family Status: single.

178. Carreras, Jose. Page 34. Occupation: farmer. Origin: Minorca. Family Status: wife and 2 children. Other: in 1786 as Joseph Carreres, age 31 (Mills 1992). (Josep Carreres, Mahon, Minorca, Rasico 1990: 159).

179. Llopis, Bartholome. Page 34. Occupation: farmer. Origin: Minorca. Family Status: wife and 2 children. Other: (Bartomeu Llopis, Alayor Minorca, farmer, fisherman, sailor; Rasico 1990:162). As Bartolomé Lopis, in a memorial of July 12, 1784, requests recognition as a natural-born subject (Lockey 1949:233).

180. Megy, Francisco. Page 34. Origin: Mahon, Minorca. Family Status: married with 2 sons and 2 daughters.

181. Prat, Jaime de. Page 34. Occupation: farmer. Origin: Minorca. Family Status: wife and son. Other: in 1787 as Jayme Prais (Mills 1992). (Jaume Prats, Alayor Minorca; Rasico 1990:165). As Santiago Prats, in a memorial of July 12, 1784, requests recognition as a natural-born subject (Lockey 1949:233).

182. Baillon, Ysaac. Page 35. Origin: Georgia. Family Status: widower.

183. Black, David. Page 35. Origin: Scotland. Family Status: widower. Other: "He lives in the house of Mistress Ward."

184. Kerr, Alan. Page 35. Occupation: cooper. Origin: Pennsylvania. Family Status: single.

185. Marchal, Manuel. Page 35. Origin: Malta. Family Status: wife and son. Other: in 1787 as Manuel Marzail (Mills 1992).

186. Moises, David. Page 35. Occupation: store (and warehouse for tanners [*almagacen de teneros*]) on Carlota street. Origin: Poland. Family Status: single. Other: "Intends to leave within the time

limits for British territory." Has a white boy in his warehouse and rents two slaves. As David Moses, signed Address from the British Subjects thanking Governor Zespedes "with the warmest acknowledgement and thanks for security and tranquility afforded us ... during the whole course of the Evacuation," dated 24th of March 1785 (Lockey 1949: 532-533). Jewish.

187. OLeary, Derby. Page 35. Occupation: shopkeeper for distilled liquor. Origin: Ireland. Family Status: single. Other: in 1784 intends to remain in East Florida.

188. Scotland, Jacobo. Page 35. Occupation: trader in wines. Origin: Scotland. Family Status: wife and children.

189. Tuffts [or Tuhis], Simon. Page 35. Occupation: merchant and auctioneer. Origin: Boston. Family Status: single. Other: He lives in the custodian residence of Henderson. Simon Tuffts signed the Address from the British Subjects thanking Governor Zespedes "with the warmest acknowledgement and thanks for security and tranquility afforded us ... during ... the Evacuation," dated 24th of March 1785 (Lockey 1949: 532-533).

190. English, Roberto. Page 36. Occupation: farmer. Origin: Ireland. Family Status: widower and 5 children.

191. Fowis, Juan. Page 36. Occupation: without any. Origin: Scotland. Family Status: single.

192. Kelly, Jose. Page 36. Occupation: shoemaker. Origin: Ireland. Family Status: wife and 2 children. Other: In 1784 intends to remain in East Florida.

193. Marran, David (in 1784 spelt "Marrant"). Page 36. Occupation: bartender. Origin: Ireland. Family Status: wife and son sent to Georgia. Other: In 1784 intends to remain in East Florida.

194. Robertson, Enrique. Page 36. Occupation: trader. Origin: Scotland. Family Status: wife.

195. Stewart, Matheo. Page 36. Occupation: chairmaker. Origin: Ireland. Family Status: wife and son. Other: "Three houses from that of Colonel Brown."

196. Warington, Nicolas. Page 36. Occupation: tailor. Origin: England. widower and 3 daughters. Other: As Nicholas Warrington, signed Address from the British Subjects thanking Governor Zespedes "with the warmest acknowledgement and thanks for security and tranquility afforded us ... during the whole course of the Evacuation," dated 24th of March 1785 (Lockey 1949: 532-533).

197. Chanela, Jose. Page 37. Occupation: tailor. Origin: Italy. Family Status: wife

198. Doemis, Carlos. Page 37. Occupation: captain of ship and pilot. Origin: Ireland. Family Status: wife and 3 children.

199. Grigly, Ricardo. Page 37. Origin: South Carolina.

200. Mason, Ysabel. Page 37. Origin: Germany. Family Status: widow.

201. Reynolds, Juan. Page 37. Occupation: merchant. Origin: Ireland. Family Status: single. Other: intends to leave.

202. Smith, Jacobo. Page 37. Occupation: cashier of commercial house. Origin: England. Family Status: single. Other: has "white woman known as Isabel Cook and also another called Ana Cameron. These degenerates [*degragados*] are without any doubt destined for the British Domains. In his profession as cashier of a commercial house he lives in a house on Carlota street belonging to the said Isabel Cook and also has a female slave."

203. Tweed, Catalina. Page 37. Occupation: lives on her savings. Origin: Scotland. Family Status: widow, 3 children. Other: "She lives in the house of Captain Brown."

204. Deewalt, Daniel. Page 38. Occupation: farmer. Origin: Pennsylvania. Family Status: wife and 2 children.

205. Depuy, Isac. Page 38. Origin: England. Family Status: wife and children.

206. Imry, Juan [spelt Imrie in 1784]. Page 38. Occupation: ship builder. Origin: Scotland. Family Status: Italian wife and 2 children. Other: in 1786 of the Catholic religion, has two canoes with six oars (Mills 1992).

207. Maxwell, Guilermo. Page 38. Occupation: architect, builder of machines (*constructor maquinista*) and in the war had been assistant engineer of the former British government. Origin: England. Family Status: widower and son. Other: In 1784 intends to remain in East Florida. There is a paper, dated April 1, 1785, in the East Florida collection listed as "observations of William Maxwell (card index of the East Florida collection"). As William Maxwell, signed Address from the British Subjects thanking Governor Zespedes "with the warmest acknowledgment and thanks for security and tranquillity afforded us ... during the whole course of the Evacuation," dated 24th of March 1785 (Lockey 1949: 532-533).

208. Milor, Carlos. Page 38. Occupation: painter and installer of glass windows. Origin: Germany. Other: "He lives in the house of Juan Flanagan." He wants to remain in the country if permitted to bring wife and children from Charleston.

209. Mofet, Roberto. Page 38. Occupation: maker of carriages and tavern owner. Origin: England. Other: "He lives with the previous mentioned Maxwell." Robert Muffett is one of the signers of an "Address of the Principal Inhabitants to Governor Tonyn" of June 6, 1783 (Lockey 1949:115).

210. Barnes, Jorge. Page 39. Occupation: merchant. Origin: Ireland. Family Status: wife and son. Other: "George Barnes & Co." is one of the signers of an Address of the British Subjects, dated on the 15th of February of 1785, seeking a prolongation of the stipulated term of residence . (Lockey 1949:521-522). As George Barnes signed Address from the British Subjects thanking Governor Zespedes

"with the warmest acknowledgement and thanks for security and tranquility afforded us ... during the whole course of the Evacuation," dated 24th of March 1785 (Lockey 1949: 532-533).

211. Cañon, Rusero. Page 39. Occupation: farmer. Origin: Georgia. Family Status: single. Other: left leave East Florida.

212. Cornic, Jose. Page 39. Occupation: carpenter. Origin: Georgia. Other: He lives in the house of Jose Pons."

213. Fox, Benjamin. Page 39. Occupation: farmer. Origin: South Carolina. Family Status: single. Other: He lived with Rusero Cañon. Other: left East Florida.

214. Kerr, Jorje. Page 39. Occupation: commerce, in 1784- merchant. Origin: Georgia. Family Status: single. Other: companion of Jorje Barnes. George Ker is one of the signers of a "Memorial and Petition of the Inhabitants of East Florida" of September 11, 1783 (Lockey 1949:158).

215. Buderfort, Jacobo. Page 40. Occupation: sailor. Origin: Georgia. Family Status: single. Other: "He lives in the house of Alejandro Paterson."

216. Johnson, Guillermo. Page 40. Occupation: pilot. Origin: Scotland. Family Status: wife and 3 children.

217. Marshall, Juan. Page 40. Occupation: master of ship called the Black Fish. Origin: Scotland. Family Status: wife. Other: "He lives next to the house of Roque Leonor."

218. Paterson, Alejandro. Page 40. Origin: Scotland. Family Status: wife, 2 children, 2 orphans. Other: "He lives next to the house of Lorenzo Yabes."

219. Taylor, Jacobo. Page 40. Occupation: sailor and auctioneer. Origin: Scotland. James Taylor is one of the signers of a "Memorial and Petition of the Inhabitants of East Florida" of September 11, 1783 (Lockey 1949:158). James Taylor signed the Address of the

British Subjects, dated on the 15th of February of 1785, seeking a prolongation of the stipulated term of residence and also the Address from the British Subjects thanking Governor Zespedes "with the warmest acknowledgement and thanks for security and tranquility afforded us ... during ... the Evacuation," dated 24th of March 1785 (Lockey 1949: 521-522, 532-533).

220. Jones, Thomas. Pages 40 -41. occupation: sailing master. Origin: Georgia. Family Status: wife and 2 children. Other: In 1784 intends to remain in East Florida.

221. Lorimer, Alexandro. Page 41. Occupation: merchant. Origin: Scotland. Family Status: single. Other: He has two white boys called Jacob Black and Neal Macguin. Alexander Lorimer signed the Address of the British Subjects, dated on the 15th of February of 1785, seeking a prolongation of the stipulated term of residence and also the Address from the British Subjects thanking Governor Zespedes "with the warmest acknowledgement and thanks for security and tranquility afforded us ... during the whole course of the Evacuation," dated 24th of March 1785 (Lockey 1949: 521-522, 532-533).

222. Pool, Ricardo. Page 41. Occupation: ship's carpenter. Origin: England. Family Status: wife and 2 children. Other: staying in East Florida.

223. Samson, Jacobo. Page 41. Occupation: grocer. Origin: Ireland. Family Status: wife and 2 daughters. Other: in 1784 intends to remain in East Florida.

224. Terbert, Jose. Page 41. Origin: England. Family Status: wife and son. Other: left East Florida on November 8th.

225. Newberry, Enrique. Pages 41-42. Occupation: merchant. Origin: England. Family Status: wife. Other: has own ship. Rents a house on Carlota street.

226. Lowther, Jacobo. Page 42. Occupation: sailor. Origin: England. Family Status: wife.

227. MacDonal, Jacobo. Page 42. Occupation: cashier of business. Origin: Scotland. Family Status: single.

228. Mercer, Juan. Page 42. Occupation: shoemaker. Origin: North Carolina. Family Status: single.

229. Michi, Carlos. Page 42. Occupation: merchant. Origin: Scotland. Family Status: single.

230. Simpson, Thomas. Page 42. Occupation: carpenter. Origin: North Carolina. Family Status: wife and son.

231. Delegall, Sara. Pages 42-43. Origin: Georgia. Family Status: widow. Other: sailing boat, married and left with Juan Watkins.

232. Armstrong, Fleetwood. Page 43. Occupation: wine merchant. Origin: Ireland. Family Status: wife and son. Other: "left East Florida together with Juan Hudson Irish." Fleetwood Armstrong signed the "Memorial and Petition of the Inhabitants of East Florida" of September 11, 1783 (Lockey 1949:158).

233. Begbie, Alexandro. Page 43. Occupation: merchant. Origin: Scotland. Family Status: single. Other: "He lives in the house of Juan Dobleow." Alexander Begbie signed the "Memorial and Petition ..." of September 11, 1783 (Lockey 1949:158).

234. Fowler, Jacobo. Page 43. Occupation: cooper. Origin: Scotland. Family Status: single. Other: "He lives in the house of Malcomo Ross." He left East Florida.

235. Nix, Eduardo. Page 43. Occupation: shoemaker. Origin: Virginia. Family Status: single. Other: "He lives in the house of Malcomo Ross."

236. Rigby, Thomas. Page 43. Occupation: blacksmith. Origin: England. Family Status: wife and 2 children. Other: Thomas Rigby is one of the signers of an Address of the British Subjects, dated on the

15th of February of 1785, seeking a prolongation of the stipulated term of residence . (Lockey 1949:521-522).

237, Cunningham, Alexandro. Page 44. Occupation: cooper. Origin: Scotland. Family Status: wife and widowed sister-in-law. Other: "He rents in front of habitation of Don Yesefes." He left East Florida.

238. Fox, Juan. Page 44. Occupation: merchant. Origin: Georgia. Family Status: single. Other: "He lives with the secretary of the former governor [Don Pedro Edwards]." Other: John Fox signed the Address of the British Subjects, dated on the 15th of February of 1785, seeking a prolongation of the stipulated term of residence . (Lockey 1949:521-522).

239. Masux, Christobal. Page 44. Occupation: baker. Origin: Prussia or Persia [*Pursia*]. Family Status: single. Other: "He lives in the house of Bernardo Honbart, master baker."

240. Tennant, Juan. Page 44. Occupation: gardener. Origin: Scotland. Family Status: wife and 4 children. Other: "He lives in front of where lives the English governor [Tonyn]."

241. Wallace, Jacobo. Page 44. Occupation: captain of a sloop. Origin: Scotland. Family Status: wife and 5 children.

242. Burns, Jacobo. Page 45. Occupation: windlass operator ("tornero"). Origin: Pennsylvania. Family Status: wife.

243. Cressel, Jorge. Page 45. Occupation: carpenter. Germany. Family Status: wife and 2 children. Other: in 1784 intends to remain in East Florida.

244. Curtis, Guillermo. Page 45. Occupation: tailor. Origin: Virginia. Family Status: wife.

245. Tweedy, Thomas. Page 45. Occupation: tailor. Origin: Italy. Family Status: wife and 2 children.

246. Waters, Thomas. Page 45. Occupation: grocer. Origin:

England. Family Status: wife and 2 children. Other: "He lives in front of Mistress Perpal." Thomas Waters is one of the signers of an Address of the British Subjects, dated on the 15th of February of 1785, seeking a prolongation of the stipulated term of residence. (Lockey 1949:521-522).

247. Flanagan, Miguel. Pages 45-46. Occupation: herbalist (*exercer la acedecina*), in 1784 listed as physician. Origin: Ireland. Family Status: widower. Other: "He lives in the house of Juan Flanagan." In 1784 he intends to remain in East Florida. He lost his documents in a shipwreck "on this sandbank" when coming from Charleston.

248. Clarke, Jacobo. Page 46. Occupation: innkeeper. Origin: Scotland. Family Status: wife and attached orphan. Other: In 1784 intends to remain in East Florida.

249. Pau, Jacinto. Page 46. Occupation: sailor and blacksmith. Origin: Minorca. Other: "He lives with an aunt." "Petition signed by [Jacinto Pau]. I live with an aunt of mine in El Blof. ... occupation is blacksmith and sailor and in the last war went to Havana where they arrested [me] and placed [me] on the San Luis from where I was transferred to the Santa Rosalia. From this frigate I escaped and in company with two others deserted with a canoe. And three leagues from Havana we seized a small sloop which had two white men, a boy and a black. We put the said whites and boy ashore on the coast and went with the sloop and the Black to this port where the Black and sloop were declared prizes [*buena presa*]. And now the said Pau presents himself without any compulsion and confesses his guilt and asks for pardon from the Governor in virtue of the last treaty of peace and the pardon of His Majesty conceded in celebration of the happy birth of twins by the princess. The said Pau did not present [this petition directly] because he was outside of the Spanish lands." In 1787 as Jaimio Pau, sailor and employed in an ironworks [*herreria*] (Mills 1992). (Jacint Pau, Mahon, Minorca; Rasico 1990: 164).

250. Thomas, Juan. Page 46. Occupation: farmer. Origin: Virginia. Family Status: wife and 4 children.

251. Chenoble, Ana Maria. Page 47. Occupation: seamstress in 1784. Origin: Georgia. Family Status: abandoned by husband Jorje Wuish, who was said to have married previously in England. See also entry #259. Other: His house is next to the Italian Riccio. In 1784 he intends to remain in East Florida.

252. Cox, Thomas. Page 47. Occupation: tailor. Origin: South Carolina. Family Status: wife and daughter.

253. Hollinsworth, Timoteo. Page 47. Occupation: "associated with the ships near where he lives." Origin: North Carolina. Family Status: wife and 5 children. Other: As Timothy Hollingirth, is one of the signers of Address of the Inhabitants of the River St. John of 25th of January 1785 (Lockey 1949:471). In 1787 listed as a farmer (Mills 1992).

254. MacClearan, Guillermo. Page 47. Occupation: has a bar (*aguardenteria*) "which he rents." Origin: Ireland. Family Status: single. Other: "He lives in the house of Mr. Clarke."

255. Allen, Thomas [written as "Hallen" in 1784]. Pages 47-48. Occupation: sailor. Origin: Scotland. Family Status: wife and white female apprentice seamstress. Other: "The wife of this individual, Cathalina, previously married (*nuncias* in text = *nupcias*) to Juan Tunkley, who left her in his will an island of 50 acres of land one mile from the fort of Matanzas and another 250 acres seven miles to the south of the expressed island, all of which can be proven with verified documents." In 1784 he intends to remain in East Florida.

256. Curtis, Benjamin. Page 48. Occupation: carpenter. Origin: Boston. Family Status: widower. Other: He shares lodging with Juan Holland.

257. Marshall, Juan. Page 48. Occupation: carpenter. Origin: England. Other: In 1784 intends to remain in East Florida.

258. Sims, Guillermo. Page 48. Occupation: silversmith. Origin: Scotland. Family Status: wife and son.

259. Vish, Jorje. Page 48. "Providencia" (Providence Rhode Island or New Providence island in the Bahamas). See also entry # 251. Other: Married with Ana Marion Chenoble and alleges that she is a woman with a "bad life."

260. Waters, Sinclair. Page 48. Occupation: tailor. Origin: Scotland. Family Status: wife, who has separated from him, and a son. Lives with an Englishman called Davins Wansey. Declared on the 18th of January that had not sold three slaves to Derby O Leary.

261. Slater, Guillermo. Pages 48-49. Occupation: merchant and public auctioneer. Origin: England. Family Status: wife and 2 children. Other: William Slater is one of the signers of an Address of the British Subjects, dated on the 15th of February of 1785, seeking a prolongation of the stipulated term of residence. (Lockey 1949:521-522). As William Slater, signed Address from the British Subjects thanking Governor Zespedes "with the warmest acknowledgement and thanks for security and tranquility afforded us ... during the whole course of the Evacuation," dated 24th of March 1785 (Lockey 1949: 532-533).

262. Fuerson, Samuel. Page 49. Occupation: tanner, chairmaker and saddler. Origin: Ireland. Family Status: single but includes Juan Baily, a nephew called Roberto Uerlin and an apprentice named David Duncan.

263. Henar, Esteban [in 1784 spelt Henat]. Page 49. Occupation: carpenter. Origin: France. Family Status: wife. Other: in 1784 intends to remain in East Florida.

264. Lord, Benjamin. Page 49. Occupation: former head surveyor of the province. Origin: England. Family Status: wife and 5 children. Other: left East Florida. Benjamin Lord signed the "Address of the Principal Inhabitants to Governor Tonyn" of June 6, 1783 (Lockey

1949:115). Mowat (1964:163) identifies him as Surveyor General from 1782-1785.

265. Stage, Federico. Page 49. Occupation: baker. Saxony (Germany). Family Status: wife and son. Other: in 1784 intends to remain in East Florida.

266. Curtis, Guillermo. Pages 49-50. Occupation: lives on his savings. Origin: England. Other: " He lives next to the house of Mister Newberry on Carlota street."

267. Broddy, Juan. Page 50. Occupation: tailor. Origin: Scotland. Family Status: single. Other: "He lives with master tailor Warrington[19] on the plaza."

268. Burgess, Thomas. Page 50. Occupation: shoemaker. Origin: Ireland. Family Status: widower. Other: "makes the best boots in the country." Other: In 1784 intends to remain in East Florida.

269. Cordery, Thomas. Page 50. Occupation: butcher. Origin: Pennsylvania. Family Status: wife and 4 children. Other: in 1786, Protestant, age 64 (Mills 1992).

270. Deveu [or Devert or David], Andres. Page 50. Occupation: painter and installer of glass. Origin: Ireland. Family Status: single.

271. Fagan, Jacobo. Page 50. Occupation: farmer. Origin: Ireland. Family Status: single. Other: In 1784 intends to remain in East Florida.

272. Flanagan, Juan. Page 50. Occupation: gunsmith and cutler. Origin: Ireland. Family Status: wife and 2 children. Other: his brother in law is holding seven slaves for him in the United States.

273. More, Thomas. Page 50. Occupation: meat chopper. Origin: Ireland. Family Status: single. with attached wife and one son.

---

[19]Nick Warrington was one of the signers of the "Address of the Principal Inhabitants to Governor Tonyn" of June 6, 1783 (Lockey 1949:115).

274. Henderson, Susana. Page 51. Occupation: seamstress. Origin: South Carolina. Family Status: widow. Other: intends to remain in East Florida.

275. Hor, Ponsi. Page 51. Occupation: carpenter. Origin: "New Scotland." Family Status: single. Other: ill, lives on charity.

276. More, Dorotea. Page 51. Occupation: lives on her savings. Origin: Ireland. Family Status: widow and 2 children.

277. Piles, Juan. Page 51. Origin: South Carolina. Other: crossed out in original manuscript.

278. Macleod, Rodrigo. Page 52. Occupation: shopkeeper. Origin: Scotland. Family Status: single. Other: "He lives near the house of Panton."

279. Macpheal, Margarita. Page 52. Occupation: seamstress in 1784. Origin: native of this city. Family Status: unmarried single woman. Other: Thomas Tweedy lost the documents of a house of her's that he occupies and claims. David Turnbull declared that the house and house lot of this orphan was bought by her father from a free Spanish black.

280. Macquin, Alexandro. Page 52. Occupation: dried foods grocer. Origin: Scotland. Family Status: wife and 3 children. Other: Don Thomas Orr sends off two slaves belonging to him.

281. Montel, Antonio. Page 52. Occupation: cashier for seaborne commerce. Origin: England. Family Status: wife and 2 children. Other: "He lives near the house of Bernardo Quni."

282. Cade, Juan. Page 53. Occupation: school master. Origin: Virginia. Family Status: wife and son. Other: "lost in America the ranch that he had."

283. Cuthbert, Jacobo. Page 53. Occupation: lives on his savings. Origin: Scotland. Family Status: single. Other: "He lives in the house of Mistress Cook on Carlota street."

284. Ficher, Juan. Page 53. Occupation: poultry merchant. Origin: Scotland. Family Status: single. Other: "He lives in front of the residence of Moises the Jew."

285. Halberto, Juan. Page 53. Occupation: dried foods grocer. Origin: Scotland. Family Status: single. Other: "He lives in store attached to the house of Moises the Jew."

286. Piles, Sara. Page 53. Origin: England. Family Status: widow and 2 children. Other: "He lives next to the house of Mistress Perpal."

287. Weaver, John. Page 53. Origin: Pennsylvania. Other: a private in the militia.

288. Mitchell, Juan. Pages 53-54. Origin: Scotland. Family Status: wife and 4 children. Other: "He lives on the street of Master Flix." As John Mitchell, he signed the Address thanking Governor Zespedes "with the warmest acknowledgement and thanks for security and tranquility afforded us ... during the whole course of the Evacuation," dated 24th of March 1785 (Lockey 1949: 532-533).

289. Beggby, Guillermo. Page 54. Occupation: ship's carpenter. Origin: Scotland. Family Status: single.

290. Crawford, Thomas. Page 54. Origin: Scotland. Family Status: single. Other: "He lives in the house of Maestro Gualtero Blando in front of the house of Maestro Fatio."

291. Porter, Rosa. Page 54. Occupation: sold drinks. shopkeeper in 1784. Origin: Ireland. Family Status: husband absent.

292. Turnbull, David. Page 54. Occupation: tanner and shoemaker. Origin: Scotland. Family Status: wife and 3 children. Other: in 1784 intends to stay in East Florida.

293. Clarkson, Maria. Pages 54-55. Origin: South Carolina. Family Status: widow. Other: "She lives with her grandmother in the house of Don Carlos Laun."

294. Ashton, Eduardo. Page 55. Occupation: tailor. Origin: Ireland. Family Status: widower and 5 children. Other: In 1786, Catholic, age 38 (Mills 1992).

295. Freemantle, Samuel. Page 55. Occupation: tailor. Origin: England. Family Status: wife and 2 children. Other: left East Florida.

296. Kertlan, Guillermo. Page 55. Occupation: farmer. Origin: Maryland. Family Status: single. Other: left East Florida.

297. Pobey, Ricardo. Page 55. Occupation: saddler. Origin: England. Family Status: single. Other: "He lives in the house of Josef Weaver."

298. Robertson, Enrique. Page 55. Origin: England. Other: "He lives in the house of Mr. Hopkins."

299. Hombard, Bernardo. Page 55. Occupation: baker. Origin: Alsace France. Family Status: wife and children. Other: owns three houses and has a very good servant. Barnard Humbard is one of the signers of an "Address of the Principal Inhabitants to Governor Tonyn" of June 6, 1783 (Lockey 1949:115).

300. Robinson, Juan. Page 55. Occupation: tailor. Origin: Ireland. Family Status: wife and 2 children.

301. Manen, Eduardo. Pages 55-56. Occupation: mason. Origin: England. Family Status: wife and 4 children.

302. Harrison, Juan. Page 56. Occupation; none but in 1784 listed as a clerk. Origin: Ireland. Family Status: widower. Other: He lives in front of the house of Master Fiche." In 1784 he intends to remain in East Florida.

303. Johnson, Juan. Page 56. Occupation: agent for a small town. Origin: Scotland. Family Status: single. Has a white servant called Hubo Macan. Other: John Johnson is one of the signers of an "Address of the Principal Inhabitants to Governor Tonyn" of June 6, 1783 (Lockey 1949:115). John Johnson is one of the signers of an

Address of the British Subjects, dated on the 15th of February of 1785, seeking a prolongation of the stipulated term of residence. (Lockey 1949:521-522).

304. Ward, Juana. Page 56. Occupation: laundress and seamstress. Origin: Scotland. widow and 3 children. Other: "He lives in house belonging to her sister."

305. Watkins, Juan. Page 56. Occupation: farmer. Origin: England. Family Status: single. Other: "He had in his house a lady called Marran who left for Charleston."

306. Wauer, Jose. Page 56. Occupation: ship's carpenter. Origin: Pennsylvania. Family Status: wife and 4 children. Has added a white boy called Thomas Eleonor. Other: He lives in front of the house of Master Fiche."

307. Zubly, David. Page 56. Occupation: auctioneer and school master. Origin: South Carolina. Family Status: wife and 2 children.

308. Backhouse, Jorje. Page 57. Occupation: tailor. Origin: England. Family Status: single. Other: Listed in 1787 (but NOT in the 1784 manuscript) as Jorje Backhayse a native of the East Indies who wants to remain in East Florida (see Mills 1992:56). Aron Dickson indicated as part of household.

309. Cameron, Donaldo. Page 57. Occupation: sailor. Origin: Scotland. Family Status: wife, sister and mother. Other: Donald Cameron signed the "Memorial and Petition of the Inhabitants of East Florida" of September 11, 1783 and the Address of the British Subjects, of the 15th of February of 1785, seeking a prolongation of the stipulated term of residence, (Lockey 1949:158, 521-522).

310. Duncan, Guillermo. Page 57. Occupation: gardener. Origin: Scotland. Family Status: wife. Other: "He lives in front of the house of Don Carlos Howard."[20]

---

[20]There is a note from Carlos Howard, dated December 12, 1784, in the East Florida papers (card index, East Florida papers).

311. Holland, Juan. Page 57. Occupation: mason and stonecutter. Origin: England. Family Status: wife and 2 children.

312. Love, Juan. Page 57. Origin: England. Family Status: wife and 2 children.

313. MacFarlan, Juan. Page 57. Occupation: "store merchant." Origin: Scotland. Family Status: single.

314. Macragh, Felipe. Page 57. Occupation: tailor. Origin: Scotland. Family Status: wife and son. Other: "has an apprentice boy known as Maclenan."

315. Anderson, Tomas. Page 58. Occupation: carpenter. Origin: England. Family Status: wife and 4 children.

316. Bona, Guillermo. Page 58. Occupation: sailor. Origin: Ireland. Family Status: married outside of the province. Other: "is master of a schooner registered in this province."

317. DeWaldt, Pedro. Page 58. Origin: Pennsylvania. Family Status: single. Other: left for the United States.

318. Moor, Francisco. Page 58. Occupation: sailor. Origin: New York. Family Status: wife. Other: left East Florida

319. Moor, Juan. Page 58. Occupation: wool or hide cleaner (*tinero*). Origin: New York. Family Status: wife. Other: left East Florida.

320. Shever, Judith. Page 58. Origin: Virginia. Family Status: widow and 5 daughters. Other: "She lives in the house of Field Marshal Tonyn.[21]"

321. Smith, Ana. Page 58. Origin: South Carolina. Family Status: widow and 3 children. Other: left province

---

[21]Tonyn was a Major General in the English Army (Tanner 1989:60). The title "Field Marshal" is not applied to him in the published literature.

322. Smart, Ysac. Pages 58-59. Occupation: stonecutter. Origin: North Carolina.

323. Boyes, Isabel. Page 59. Occupation: tailor and seamstress. Origin: Georgia. Family Status: widow, daughter, little sister. Also an old white person called Margarita Meyrhaven. Other: in 1787 as Boyce (Mills 1992).

324. Christie, Maria. Page 59. Origin: South Carolina. Family Status: widow and 3 children.

325. Coin, Benjamin. Page 59. Occupation: farmer. Origin: South Carolina. Family Status: wife and son.

326. Cox, Carlos. Page 59. Occupation: ship's carpenter. Origin: England. Family Status: wife and 2 children. Other: left East Florida.

327. Hewitt, Sara. Page 59. Origin: England. Family Status: widow and 2 daughters. Other: left East Florida.

328. Mackenzie, Daniel. Page 59. Occupation: carpenter. Origin: Georgia. Family Status: single. Other: "He lives in the house of the widow Smith above the bay."

329. Tudy, Jacobo. Pages 59-60. Occupation: blacksmith and locksmith. Origin: Germany. Family Status: wife, son, two apprentices and an orphan. Other: left East Florida.

330. Anthrobus, Juan. Page 60. Occupation: farmer. Origin: England. Family Status: single. Other: "He lives with his brother in law Isac Dupuy."

331. Cupsted, Juan. Page 60. Occupation: farmer. Origin: South Carolina. Family Status: wife. Other: "He lives in the house of the previously cited Jacobo." Other: left East Florida.

332. Guy, Jacobo. Page 60. Occupation: keeper of firewood (*contador de leña*). Origin: South Carolina. Family Status: single. Other: "He lives in the house of David Hodge."

333. Leslie, Josef. Page 60. Occupation: farmer. Origin: South Carolina. Family Status: wife. Other: "He lives with Isac Dupuy."

334. Lewis, Jacobo. Page 60. Occupation: butcher. Origin: England. Family Status: single. Other: "He lives in the house of Jacobo Ohuli."

335. Manus, Nazaniel. Page 60. Occupation: farmer. Origin: Virginia. Family Status: single. Other: "He lives in the house of Isac Dupuy." Other: in 1784 intends to remain in East Florida.

336. Taylor, David. Page 60. Occupation: baker. Origin: Scotland. Family Status: wife.

337. Wales, Jacobo. Page 60. Occupation: baker. Origin: England. Family Status: wife and 2 children. Other: "He lives in house on Carlota street next to [that of] Dona Ororia Carguel."

338. Cooper, Isabel. Pages 60-61. Occupation: seamstress. Origin: England. Family Status: married. Has a son that lives with her. Separated from her husband, who lives in town, because of his bad treatment of her. Other: in 1784 intends to remain in East Florida.

339. English, Juan. Page 61. Occupation: fisherman. Origin: England. Family Status: wife and son. Other: left East Florida.

340. Green, Guillermo. Page 61. Occupation: ship's carpenter. Origin: South Carolina. Other: "He lives with the German Grassel" [Grassel was one of the signers of the "Memorial" of September 11, 1783, Lockey 1949:158]. Other: left East Florida.

341. Jones, Guillermo. Page 61. Occupation: carpenter. Origin: North Carolina. Family Status: single. Other: "Lives in the house of the German carpenter Grassel."

342. Miguins, Juan. Page 61. Occupation: ship's carpenter. Origin: England. Family Status: wife and 3 children. Other: "He lives two doors from Lorenzo Yanes."

343. Robinson, Francisco. Page 61. Occupation: ship's carpenter. Origin: Scotland. Family Status: single. Other: "He lives in the house of Master Tanning [which is] next to [that of] Field Marshal Tonyn.

344. Robinson, Juana. Page 61. Occupation: seamstress. Origin: England. Family Status: widow. Other: He lives in the house of Master Hely.

345. Thompson, Thomas. Page 61. Occupation: carpenter. Origin: Scotland. Family Status: single. Other: "He lives in the house of the German carpenter Grassel."

346. Dort, Guillermo. Pages 61-62. Occupation: cashier for merchant. Origin: England. Family Status: wife and 2 children.

347. Close, Juan. Page 62. Occupation: mason. Origin: Ireland. Family Status: single. Other: in 1784 intends to remain in East Florida.

348. Crane, Spencer. Page 62. Occupation: fisherman. Origin: North Carolina. Family Status: single. Other: "He lives in the house of Juan English."

349. Kenesbach, Ysabel. Page 62. Occupation: seller of dried food (*vender tenderos secos*). Origin: Scotland. Family Status: German husband who lives in Germany.

350. Lermont, Roberto. Page 62. Occupation: baker. Origin: Scotland. Family Status: single.

351. Newell, Ana. Page 62. Occupation: seamstress in 1784, husband is a sailor. Origin: Ireland. Family Status: son. Other: in 1784 intends to remain in East Florida.

352. Tailor, Ysabel. Page 62. Occupation: laundress and seamstress. Origin: England. Family Status: widow and 2 children

353. Hopkins, Juan. Pages 62-63. Occupation: shoemaker. Origin: England. Family Status: wife. Other: in 1787 as shoemaker (Mills 1992).

354. Boland, Juan. Page 63. Occupation: shoemaker. Origin: South Carolina. Family Status: wife and 4 children.

355. Evelin, Juan. Page 63. Occupation: carpenter. Origin: England. Family Status: single. Other: "He lives in the house of Juan Holland."

356. Letson [or Lessam], Roberto Page 63. Occupation: carpenter. Origin: [New?] Jersey. Family Status: wife and 4 children. Other: "lives in the house of Colonel Monerief."

357. Paiyne, Enrique. Page 63. Origin: England. Family Status: single. Other: "He lives in the house of Juan Macfarlan next to Johnson the tavern keeper."

358. Pons, Jacobo. Page 63. Occupation: carpenter, in 1784 a trader. Origin: Virginia. Family Status: wife and son.

359. Steed, Thomas. Page 63. Occupation: butcher. Origin: England. Family Status: single. Other: "in the house of the accountant More."

360. Ross, Malcolmó. Pages 63-64. Occupation: carpenter. Origin: Scotland. Family Status: wife and son. Other: Malcom Ross is one of the signers of a "Memorial and Petition of the Inhabitants of East Florida" of September 11, 1783 (Lockey 1949:159).

361. Brown, Carlos. Page 64. Occupation: master of sloop. Origin: Scotland. Family Status: wife and 2 children. Other: "He lives in front of the house of ... Mowbray."

362. Burton, Ana. Page 64. Occupation: seamstress in 1784. Origin: Ireland. Family Status: widow. Other: "She lives in the house of Isabel Taylor." Other: in 1784 intends to stay in East Florida.

363. Davidson, Alexandro. Page 64. Occupation: experienced pilot (*platico* in text = *practico*). Origin: Scotland. Family Status: wife.

Other: on April 19th sold 2 blacks to Mr. Junno. He lives near the office of English armory.

364. Macboy, Juan. Page 64. Occupation: weaver. Origin: Ireland. Family Status: wife and 4 children. Other: "He lives in the house of Jacobo Barnit." He intends to live in Pensacola where has family; private in the militia.

365. Macphearson, Duncan. Page 64. Occupation: farmer. Origin: Scotland. Family Status: wife and 2 children. Other: " He lives in a house rented from Turnbull." He left East Florida.

366. Martin, Alexandro. Page 64. Occupation: has liquor store. Origin: Scotland. Family Status: wife and 4 children. Other: He left East Florida.

367. Reed, Roberto. Page 64. Occupation: farmer. Origin: Scotland. Family Status: single. Other: "He lives in house near that of Mistress Claguer." "He has a white overseer called Luis Obrien."

368. Ferre, Juan. Page 65. Occupation: farmer and fisherman. Origin: Minorca. Family Status: wife. Other: 22 years old. (Joan Ferrer, Mahon, Minorca; Rasico 1990:161). In 1787 as Juan Ferri (Mills 1992).

369. Pedro de Bordo, Pepe. Page 65. Occupation: shopkeeper. Origin: Corsica. Family Status: single. Other: in 1787 as Pepino Pedro de Burgo (Mills 1992). Francesco Pesso di Borgo in a memorial of July 12, 1784, requests recognition as a natural-born subject (Lockey 1949:232). As Francisco Pozo de Borgo listed in the Petition of the Italians and Greeks of the 27th of January 1787 (Lockey 1949:463).

370. Pelegrin, Bartolome. Page 65. Occupation: sailor. Origin: Minorca. Family Status: wife and son. Other: (Bartomeu Pelegri; Rasico 1990: 164). In 1786, age 22 (Mills 1992).

371. Theo, Antonio. Page 65. Occupation: farmer. Origin: Minorca. Family Status: widower with daughter.

372. Trian, Juan. Page 65. Occupation: stonecutter. Origin: Minorca. Family Status: wife and son.

373. Triay, Juan. Page 65. Occupation: farmer and fisherman. Origin: Minorca. Family Status: wife and 3 children. Other: (Joan Triay, Ciudadela Minorca; Rasico 1990: 168).

374. Arnau, Bernardo. Page 66. Occupation: farmer. Origin: Minorca. Family Status: wife and son. Other: in 1786, age 36 (Mills 1992). (Bernat Arnau, San Felipe, Minorca, farmer, sailor; Rasico 1990:158). As Bernat Harnau, in a memorial of July 12, 1784, requests recognition as a natural-born subject (Lockey 1949:233).

375. Barti, Antonio. Page 66. Occupation: farmer and blacksmith. Origin: Minorca. Family Status: wife and 5 children.

376. Berbe, Juan. Page 66. Occupation: fisherman. Origin: Minorca. Family Status: single. Other: "He lives with Juan Ferre."

377. Caravach, Jose. Page 66. Occupation: farmer. Origin: "Greek Nation." Family Status: single. Other: "He lives with Juan Chonopla."

378. Columinas, Juan. Page 66. Occupation: linen weaver. Origin: Barcelona. Family Status: wife. (Joan Colomines, sailmaker; Rasico 1990:160). Other: Juan Columynas in a memorial of July 12, 1784, requests recognition as a natural-born subject (Lockey 1949:232).

379. Estefanople, Jorje. Page 66. Occupation: farmer. Origin: Corsica. Family Status: single. Other: in 1787 as overseer (Mills 1992).

380. Mir, Antonio. Page 66. Occupation: farmer and fisherman. Origin: Minorca. Family Status: wife and son. (Antoni Mir, Alayor Minorca; Rasico 1990: 163).

381. Roger, Roberto. Page 66. Occupation: carpenter. Origin: Minorca. Family Status: wife and daughter. Other: As Roberto

Roger in a memorial of July 12, 1784, requests recognition as a natural-born subject (Lockey 1949:233).

382. Sabater, Pablo. Page 66. Occupation: fisherman and farmer. Origin: Minorca. Family Status: wife and son. Other: in 1787 as Pablo Sabatier (Mills 1992). (Pau Sabater, Ciudadela Minorca; Rasico 1990: 167).

383. Stoop, Pedro. Pages 66-67. Occupation: farmer. Origin: Minorca. Family Status: wife and daughter. Other: in 1787 as Pedro Stopa (Mills 1992).

384. Capelde, Luis. Page 67. Occupation: carpenter. Origin: "Infantes." Family Status: wife and 3 children.

385. Coll, Sebastian. Page 67. Occupation: carpenter. Origin: Minorca. Family Status: wife and son. Other: "He lives near Mistress Perpat." Other: in 1786, 29 years old (Mills 1992). (Mahon, Minorca; Rasico 1990: 160).

386. Hernandez, Martin. Page 67. Occupation: water edge carpenter (*de ribera*). Origin: Minorca. Family Status: wife and daughter. Other: "He lives near Mr. Fich." Other: in 1786, age 30 (Mills 1992).

387. Perpal, Ysabel. Page 67. Occupation: merchant. Origin: Minorca. 3 children. (Rasico 1990: 165). Other: Purchased land of Don Elias Ball from Don Jesse Fish (Mills 1992:52). In 1787 as farmer (Mills 1992).

388. Pons, Jose. Page 67. Occupation: farmer. Origin: Minorca. Family Status: wife and daughter. Other: 33 years old. (Josep Pons, Mahon, Minorca; Rasico 1990: 165). As Josef Pons, in a memorial of July 12, 1784, requests recognition as a natural-born subject (Lockey 1949:233).

389. Triay, Gabriel. Page 67. Occupation: carpenter. Origin: Minorca. Family Status: wife and son. Other: 30 years old. Other: in 1786, age 30 (Mills 1992). (Ciudadela Minorca; Rasico 1990:168).

390. Villalonga, Juan. Page 67. Occupation: shopkeeper. Origin: Minorca. Family Status: wife and 2 children. Other: in 1787 as farmer (Mills 1992). (Joan Villalonga, Alayor Minorca; Rasico 1990: 169). As Juan Villalonga in a memorial of July 12, 1784, requests recognition as a natural-born subject (Lockey 1949:233).

391. Lorenzo, Juan. Pages 67-68. Occupation: mason. Origin: Minorca. Family Status: wife and 3 children. Other: in 1786, bricklayer, age 31 (Mills 1992).

392. Casals, Vicente. Page 68. Occupation: carpenter. Origin: Minorca. Family Status: wife and 2 children. Other: in 1787 as Vizente Casaty (Mills 1992).

393. Estafanofa, Jorge. Page 68.

394. Garmaldo, Eulalia. Page 68. Occupation: lives on her savings. Origin: Minorca. Family Status: widow and 3 children.

395. Paseo, Pedro. Page 68. Occupation: sailor. Origin: Corsica. Family Status: wife and 2 children.

396. Solano, Manuel Page 68. Occupation: farmer. Origin: native of Florida. Family Status: wife and 2 children.

397. Vila, Francisco. Page 68. Occupation: farmer. Origin: Minorca. Family Status: wife. Other: [Francesc Vila, Mahon, Minorca; Rasico 1990: 169]. As Francisco Bila, in a memorial of July 12, 1784, requests recognition as a natural-born subject (Lockey 1949:233).

398. Alcantara, Antonio. Page 69. Occupation: sailor. Origin: Minorca. Family Status: wife and 2 children. (Rasico 1990:158)

399. Andreu, Antonio. Page 69. Occupation: carpenter. Origin: Minorca. Family Status: wife, two children and sister of wife. Other: Mercadal, Minorca (Rasico 1990:158). As Antonio Andreu, in a memorial of July 12, 1784, requests recognition as a natural-born subject (Lockey 1949:233).

400. Buchani, Jose. Page 69. Occupation: sailor. Origin: Tuscany Italy. Family Status: wife and 2 children. Other: in 1786 as Joseph Buchoni, Italy, age 39 (Mills 1992). As Josef Buchani listed in the Petition of the Italians and Greeks of the 27th of January 1787 (Lockey 1949:463).

401. Gomila, Jose. Page 69. Occupation: farmer. Origin: Minorca. Family Status: wife. Other: in 1787 as carpenter (Mills 1992). (Mahon, Minorca, carpenter, fisherman, sailor; Rasico 1990: 161).

402. Ridabert, Ylisbet. Page 69. Origin: Minorca. Family Status: unmarried woman. (Isabel Riudavets, Alayor Minorca; Rasico 1990: 166).

403. Villalonga, Antonia. Page 69. Origin: Minorca. Other: lives with sister Maria Hechol. Her sailor husband, Ambros Villaronga, has been absent (out of the province) for five years.

404, Canovas, Antonio. Page 70. Occupation: farmer. Origin: Minorca. Family Status: wife and son. Other: (Antoni Canoves, Alayor Minorca; Rasico 1990:159).

405. Ferrio, Jose. Page 70. Occupation: carpenter and farmer. Origin: France. Family Status: widower. Other: overseer and dweller on the ranch of Field Marshal [*Mariscal de Campo*] Tonyn, he owns land between the ranch of Mister Pedman and Field Marshal Tonyn.

406. Hernandez, Matheo. Page 70. Occupation: intended to be Spanish chaplain. Origin: native of San Augustine. Family Status: orphan. Other: "He lives with an English person called Watson.[22]"

407. Mestre, Antonio. Page 70. Occupation: farmer. Origin: Minorca. Family Status: widower and mother. In 1786 age 36 (Mills 1992). (Antoni Mestre, Mahon, Minorca; Rasico 1990: 163).

---

[22]William Watson is one of the signers of a "Memorial and Petition of the Inhabitants of East Florida" of September 11, 1783 (Lockey 1949:158).

408. Boneli, Jose. Page 71. Occupation: farmer. Origin: Leghorn (Italy). Family Status: wife and 3 children. Other: lives on ranch of Fatio in 1787 (Mills 1992). Giuseppe Bonelly in a memorial of July 12, 1784, requests recognition as a natural-born subject (Lockey 1949:232).

409. Flusia, Pedro. Page 71. Occupation: farmer. Origin: Minorca. Family Status: single. Other: in 1786, age 30, alternative spelling of Pedro Fezua (Mills 1992).

410. Frau, Gabriel. Page 71. Occupation: sailor. Origin: Minorca. Family Status: single. Other: lives with a sister. (fisherman, Rasico 1990: 161).

411. Maestre, Pedro. Page 71. Occupation: farmer. Origin: Minorca. Family Status: wife and 3 children. Other: in 1786, age 38.

412. Trope, Pedro. Page 71. Occupation: master of a schooner. Origin: Minorca. Family Status: wife and son. Other: Listed in the Petition of the Italians and Greeks of the 27th of January 1787 (Lockey 1949:463).

413. Yanes, Lorenzo. Page 71. Occupation: trader. Origin: native of San Augustine. Family Status: single. Other: has an English woman and [her] three children in his household.

414. Gonzales, Juan. Pages 71-72. Occupation: farmer and fisherman. Origin: Minorca. Family Status: brother, wife and son.

415. Falani, Ferdinando. Page 72. Occupation: baker. Origin: Italian. Family Status: wife and 3 children. Other: in 1787 as Ferdinando Fatany, Florence (Mills 1992). Listed in the Petition of the Italians and Greeks of the 27th of January 1787 (Lockey 1949:463).

416. Francois, Juan. Page 72. Origin: "native of Fracia [France]."

417. Llambias Antonio. Page 72. Occupation: carpenter. Origin: Mahon, Minorca. Family Status: single. Other: in 1787 as ship

carpenter (Mills 1992). (Antoni Llambies, Mahon, Minorca; Rasico 1990: 162).

418. Pyne, Diego. Page 72. Occupation: maritime and teaches navigation. Origin: Ireland. Family Status: widower. Other: "lives in one of the houses of Guillermo MacHenry."

419. Rech, Maestre. Page 72. Origin: Villanueva de Siches [Villanueva y Geltrú near Sitges and between Barcelona and Tarragona in Catalonia Spain]. Family Status: wife and daughter. Has Indian boy in household.

420. Sala, Nicolas. Page 72. Occupation: ship master. Origin: Minorca. Family Status: wife and a daughter. Other: (Nicolau Sala; Rasico 1990: 167). Listed as Nicolas Salada in Mills (1992). Nicola Salata in a memorial of July 12, 1784, requests recognition as a natural-born subject (Lockey 1949:233).

421. Stefanopoly, Antonio. Page 72. Occupation: has a schooner in which he makes trips to the United States. Origin: Corsica. Family Status: single.

422. Cobham, Don Thomas. Page 87. Occupation: physician. Origin: Scotland. Family Status: single.

423. Corbett, Don Eduardo. Page 87. Occupation: businessman. Origin: Scotland. Family Status: single. Has a white dependent known as Michael Flood. Other: "lives in the house of Don Juan Noris." As Edward Corbett he signed an Address of the British Subjects, dated on the 15th of February of 1785, seeking a prolongation of the stipulated term of residence, (Lockey 1949:521-522). He also signed the Address from the British Subjects thanking Governor Zespedes "with the warmest acknowledgement and thanks for security and tranquility afforded us ... during the whole course of the Evacuation," dated 24th of March 1785 (Lockey 1949: 532-533).

424. Yeates, Don David. Page 87. Occupation: former provincial secretary. Origin: Scotland. Family Status: wife and 4 children.

Also part of the household a white major with wife and children called Loclin Vas. Other: also spelt Yeats. Schafer (1983:111) says that David Yeats was former governor "Grant's business manager as well as a medical doctor, planter and government official." As David Yeats, he is one of the signers of an "Address of the Principal Inhabitants to Governor Tonyn" of June 6, 1783 (Lockey 1949:115). Mowat (1964:162) identifies him Deputy Secretary, Clerk of the Council, and Register of Grants, Patents, and Records.

425. Cruden, Don Juan.[23] Page 88. Occupation: businessman. Had been commissioner for the goods sequestrated [*ecuastrados*] in the provinces of South America. Origin: Scotland. Family Status: single. Other: "He lives in front of the house of Don Carlos Hobard." He left East Florida.

426. Douglas, Don Juan. Page 88. Origin: Georgia. Family Status: single with two unmarried sister. Occupation: agent for Senor Graham [Grant ?] and Senor Gale. Other: John Douglass is one of the signers of an Address of the British Subjects, dated on the 15th of February of 1785, seeking a prolongation of the stipulated term of residence. (Lockey 1949:521-522). As John Douglass signed Address from the British Subjects thanking Governor Zespedes "with the warmest acknowledgement and thanks for security and tranquility afforded us ... during the whole course of the Evacuation," dated 24th of March 1785 (Lockey 1949: 532-533).

427. Spence, Don Roberto. Page 88. Occupation: businessman. Agent for the ranch of Josiah Bagley. Origin: Scotland. Family Status: single. Other: "lives in the house of Juan Moris." He left East Florida. Robert Spence is one of the signers of an "Address of the Principal Inhabitants to Governor Tonyn" of June 6, 1783 (Lockey 1949:115).

428. Fish, Don Jesse. Pages 88-89. Origin: New York. Family Status: wife and daughter left and a son with him. Other: has a white boy

---

[23] There is a petition of "Don Juan Cruden, British American Royalist, in his name and in that of others..." dating from 12 December 1784 in the East Florida Papers (card index to the East Florida Papers).

called Enoc Barton. As Jesse Fish signed Address from the British Subjects thanking Governor Zespedes "with the warmest acknowledgement and thanks for security and tranquility afforded us ... during the whole course of the Evacuation," dated 24th of March 1785 (Lockey 1949: 532-533). Griffin (1983: 132) details the history of Jesse Fish who arrived in the first Spanish period and remained in Saint Augustine when the Spaniards returned to the city. He died in 1790. A manuscript bundle named the "accounts of Jesse Fish, 1763-1770" may be found in the East Florida papers.

429. Forbes, Dona Dorotea. Page 89. Family Status: widow and son. Other: left East Florida.

430. Levit, Don Francisco. Page 89. Occupation: farmer and [owner] of planting . Origin: Turkey. Family Status: wife and son. Other: also spelt Levett. Has a white overseer called Alexandro Beney. Francis Levett signed the "Address of the Principal Inhabitants to Governor Tonyn" of June 6, 1783 (Lockey 1949:115, 521-522) and the Address of the British Subjects, dated on the 15th of February of 1785, seeking a prolongation of the stipulated term of residence. As Francis Lovett, he signed the Address thanking Governor Zespedes "with the warmest acknowledgement and thanks for security and tranquility afforded us ... during the whole course of the Evacuation," dated 24th of March 1785 (Lockey 1949: 532-533).

431. Murray, Don Ricardo Donaban. Page 89. Occupation: In 1784 indicated as trader. Origin: Ireland. Family Status: wife. Other: in 1784 intends to stay in East Florida.

432. Leslie, Don Juan. Pages 90-91. Occupation: representative of the House of Panton, Leslie and company, in 1784 as merchant. Origin: Scotland. Agent of Adan Gordon and Don Roberto Hope. Family Status: single. Other: his partners are Panton, Forbes and MacLatchy. In San Augustine there are three dependent whites called Juan Forrester[24], Jacobo Colbert and Jacobo Gordon. Other: in

---

[24]John Forrester became a partner in 1792 and was still active in 1802 (Coker and Watson 1986:364,405).

1784 he, and his company, intends to stay in East Florida. Shipped the slaves of Don Juan Steward, the captain of the British guards. Also removed the slaves of Thomas Barrow and Carlos MacLatchy.[25]

As John Leslie, he signed the Address thanking Governor Zespedes "with the warmest acknowledgment and thanks for security and tranquillity afforded us ... during the ... Evacuation," dated 24th of March 1785 (Lockey 1949: 532-533). In 1786 he was a Protestant, age 35 (Mills 1992). Griffin (1983:132) notes he "remained in town to manage the trading interests of his firm, Panton, Leslie & Company. Bilingual and of an adaptable disposition, he was much in demand as an interpreter and arbitrator...". In the East Florida papers there is a bundle of papers "on the firm of Panton, Leslie, and Company, 1784-1813," (microfilm reel 44, bundle 116L9, container 190).

433. Garret, Don Joshuah. Page 92. Occupation: trader. Origin: North Carolina. Family Status: wife and son. Other: He lived in the "house of the old assembly."

434. MacYntosh, Don Guillermo. Page 92. Occupation: had been in charge of Indian affairs. Origin: Georgia. Family Status: single. Other: William MacIntosh signed the "Memorial and Petition" of September 11, 1783 (Lockey 1949:158).

435. Young, Don Guillermo.[26] Page 92. Occupation: early planter. Origin: Pennsylvania. Family Status: wife and son. Other: "Colonel and last Captain of a company raised to preserve the public tranquillity." Identified by Tanner (1989: 41) as "Tonyn's personal light horse troop headed by Colonel William Young."

---

[25]Charles MacLatchy was one of the signers of an "Address of the Principal Inhabitants to Governor Tonyn" of June 6, 1783 (Lockey 1949:114).

[26]The East Florida papers have "correspondence [of the governor] with Colonel Young" dating from the 14th of August 1784 (card index to the East Florida Collection).

436. Mills, Theofilo. Page 109. Occupation: planter. Origin: North Carolina. Family Status: wife and 4 children. Lives with free mulato.

437. Klepter, Juan. Page 110. Occupation: weaver. Origin: Germany. Family Status: wife and daughter. Other: "He lives in a house next to that of the Minorquin Antonio Pau."

438. Ledo, Antonio. Page 110. Origin: Portugal. Family Status: single.

439. MacCuller, Jonatan. Page 110. Occupation: farmer. Origin: South Carolina. Family Status: single. Other: "He lives with Josef MacCuller."

440. MacDaniel, Guillermo. Page 110. Occupation: merchant. Origin: Ireland. Family Status: single.

441. Macdonald, Patricio. Page 110. Occupation: silversmith. Origin: Ireland. Family Status: single. Other: "He lives with Juan Macboy."

442. Maculler, Joseph. Page 110. Occupation: farmer. Origin: South Carolina. Family Status: wife. Lives with an oldster called Tomas and a white servant called Jesse Frost.

443. Baker, Jacobo. Page 111. Occupation: sailor. Origin: England. Family Status: wife and son. Other: "lives next to the house of the Jew." Other: in 1784 intends to stay in East Florida.

444. Crosbie, Juan. Page 111. Occupation: sailor. Origin: Ireland. Family Status: single.

445. MacArthur, Juan. Page 111. Occupation: shoemaker. Origin: Ireland. Family Status: wife. Other: left East Florida.

446. Manwel, Thomas. Page 111. Occupation: sailing master. Origin: England. Family Status: wife and a son.

447. Strong, Guillermo. Page 111. Occupation: farmer. Origin: New York. Family Status: single. Other: "He lives next to the house of Mr. Hely." Other: left East Florida.

448. Taylor, Isabel. Page 111. Occupation: seamstress. Origin: Ireland. Family Status: 2 children. Husband has left. Other: "lives in the house of the shoemaker Borjeis [or Borseis]." In 1784 he intended to stay in East Florida.

449. Williams, Evan. Page 111. Occupation: sailor. Origin: England. Family Status: wife and son.

450. Hyde, Godfredo. Page 112. Occupation: sailor. Origin: Poland. Family Status: single. Other: "He lives with Juan MacArthur."

451. Johnson, Maria. Page 112. Origin: North Carolina. Family Status: widow and 6 children.

452. Jones, Ricardo. Page 112. Occupation: carpenter. Origin: Virginia. Family Status: wife and 4 children.

453. Mullegan, Sara. Page 112. Occupation: seamstress in 1784. Husband owns a schooner. Origin: England. Family Status: 2 children. Husband absent. Other: in 1784 intends to stay in East Florida. Alternative spelling is Millegan.

454. Naper, Juan. Page 112. Occupation: tailor and sells some foods. Origin: Scotland. Family Status: wife.

455. Taylor, Jose. Page 112. Occupation: gunsmith. Origin: South Carolina. Family Status: wife and son. Other: left East Florida.

456. Yarrowley [or Yallowley], Joshua. Page 112. Occupation: surveyor. Origin: England. Family Status: wife and 3 children. Other: ownes 500 acres of land above Rio San Juan.

457. Bann, Jacobo. Pages 112-113. Occupation: sailing master. Origin: England. Family Status: wife. Other: in 1784 intends to go to Pensacola where he has brothers.

458. Bailie, Juan. Page 113. Occupation: accountant. Origin: Scotland. Family Status: single. Other: "lives with Mr. Yuercon."

459. Carmichael, Jacobo. Page 113. Occupation: joiner. Origin: Scotland. Family Status: single. Other: "lives on the corner next to Mr. Levit."

460. Clarke, Juan. Page 113. Occupation: master and owner of a ship. Origin: England. Family Status: wife and 2 children.

461. Collins, Tompsy. Page 113. Family Status: her husband is away, 2 children. Occupation: husband is a butcher. Origin: Pennsylvania.

462. Ewing, Guillermo. Page 113. Occupation: farmer. Origin: Ireland. Family Status: single. Other: "He lives in the house of David Marran."

463. Fleming, Thomas. Page 113. Occupation: farmer in 1784. Origin: Scotland. Other: "He lives in the house of Alejandro Paterson." Family Status: wife and son elsewhere. Data obtained from Alejandro Paterson because he is ill with a sexual disease (*enfermo de puta*).

464. Stuard, Antonio. Page 113. Occupation: ship master. Origin: Scotland. Family Status: single. Other: "He lives in the house of Jacobo Scotland."

465, Syks, Margarita. Page 113. Origin: Virginia. Family Status: widow and son. Other: "She lives in the city with Colonel Douglas."

466. Bivins, Francisco. Page 114. Origin: England. Other: left on 25 of October.

467. Bruce, Simon. Page 114. Occupation: steward of the former governor. Origin: Brest, France. Other: "He lives in house of Jacobo Baer." He left on the October 26th.

468. Evans, Margarita. Page 114. Occupation: tailor. Origin: Pennsylvania. Family Status: widow and 5 children. Other: came to look for the relatives of her dead husband. In 1784 intends to stay in East Florida.

469. Keller, Juana. Page 114. Origin: Philadelphia [Pennsylvania]. Family Status: unmarried woman. Other: "She lives in house rented from Mistress Perpal."

470. Lapin, Maria. Page 114. Occupation: ill and lives from charity. Origin: native of America. Family Status: abandoned by her husband who returned to the United States.

471. Micky, Juan. Page 114. Occupation: ship's carpenter. Origin: Scotland. Family Status: single.

472. Motte, Jacobo. Page 114. Occupation: fisherman. Origin: North Carolina. Family Status: wife and 2 children who "live with another." Other: lives in a house rented from Mr. Pantor.

473. Brandon, Samuel. Page 115. Occupation: silversmith. Origin: Pennsylvania. Family Status: wife and 2 children. Other: "live in the house of the last named Young."

474. Hughes, Jacobo Page 115. Occupation: school master. Origin: England. Family Status: single. Other: corrected in original document from Huwe.

475. Kennedy, August [or Auguje]. Page 115. Occupation: clerk. Origin: Scotland. Family Status: single. Other: "lives in the house of Mistress More."

476. Macdonal, Lucrecia. Page 115. Origin: Pennsylvania. Other: "lives in house of Mistress Perpal next to the castle." She was "left

behind by her husband, aide de camp of General MacArthur[27], to take care of certain business."

477. Oates, Guillermo. Page 115. Occupation: has dry goods and liquor store. Origin: North Carolina. Family Status: wife and English girl and another orphan attached to his family.

478. Rees, Guillermo. Page 115. Occupation: farmer and afterwards served as an official. Origin: England. Family Status: single.

479. Young, Thomas. Page 115. Occupation: in 1784 lives on his savings. Origin: North Carolina. Family Status: widower and 5 children. Other: "He lives in house plot next to that of Mr. Cade." He sold a black to Thomas Clarke.

480. Briton, Francisco. Page 116. Occupation: sailor. Origin: England.

481. Evans, Thomas. Page 116. Occupation: sailor. Origin: England. Family Status: wife and 3 children.

482. Ryan, Juan. Page 116. Origin: Ireland.

483. Sampson, Juan. Page 116. Origin: Ireland. Family Status: wife.

484. Sims, Roberto. Page 116. Occupation: sailor. Origin: Ireland. Family Status: single. Other: "He lives in house of Juan Holland."

485. Spindler, Sebastian. Page 116. Occupation: surgeon, physician. Origin: Switzerland. Family Status: wife. Other: in 1784 intends to remain in East Florida.

486. Warner, Josiah. Page 116. Occupation: experienced pilot (*platico* in text = *practico*) for the port and coast. Origin: New York. Family Status: widower. Other: "He lives in a house of Juan Fich." In He 1784 intends to remain in East Florida.

---

[27] Brigader General Archibald MacArthur sailed for Nasseu in the Bahamas islands on August 14, 1784 (Tanner 1989:54). He was receiving letters on [New] Providence island of the Bahamas from the governor of Florida on January 17th of the following year. (card index to the East Florida papers).

487. Bennix, Thomas. Page 117. Origin: Ireland. Family Status: wife, son, mother and brother in law. Other: "He lives on the ranch of Fatil."

488. Collins, David. Page 117. Occupation: farmer, day laborer (*jornalero*). Origin: New England. Family Status: single. Other: "lives with the gunsmith Hanagan."

489. Costa, Miguel. Page 117. Occupation: physician. Origin: France. Family Status: wife. Other: "he lives near the castle with a Spaniard called Josef and speaks a little English." He intends to "leave Spanish protection in order to retire to the Mississippi." Michele Costa in a memorial of July 12, 1784, requested recognition as a natural-born subject (Lockey 1949:233).

490. Curtis, Guillermo. Page 117. Occupation: mariner. Origin: Boston (Massachusetts). Other: "He lives in the house of Jacobo Sanson."

491. Doran, Juan. Page 117. Origin: Ireland. Other: "*es guanto se la be de el por estar malo y se presenta por el medico* Don Juan Scat." See Don Roberto Scott (entry #99).

492. Mountrie, Austin. Page 117. Occupation: farmer. Origin: Virginia. Family Status: single. Other: "He lives on the Rio San Juan next to Cristobal Neely."

493. Smith, Roberto. Page 117. Origin: Scotland. Family Status: wife. Other: left East Florida.

494. Ware, Juan. Page 117. Occupation: merchant in the company of Jacobo Samson.. Origin: Ireland. Family Status: single. "lives with Jacobo Sanson." Other: left East Florida.

495. Hephensan, Jorje. Page 118. Occupation: farmer. Origin: Pennsylvania. Family Status: single.

496. Humphrys, Jacobo. Page 118. Origin: England. Family Status: single.

497. Lane, Guillermo. Page 118. Occupation: farmer. Origin: North Carolina. Family Status: single.

498. Lane, Pearce. Page 118. Occupation: farmer. Origin: North Carolina. Family Status: single.

499. Lufton, Juan. Page 118. Occupation: farmer. Origin: Virginia. Family Status: single. Other: "2nd" Juan Lufton.

500. Sutton, Beaman. Page 118. Occupation: farmer. Origin: Virginia. Family Status: single. Other: lives in the "old fields of Bell."

501. Swiney, Enrique. Page 118. Occupation: blacksmith. Origin: Virginia. Family Status: wife and 2 children. Other: "old fields of Bell."

502. Tenencys, Pedro. Page 118. Occupation: farmer. Origin: England. Other: Lives with Enrique Onell

503. Wilson, Samuel. Page 118. Origin: Pennsylvania. Family Status: single. Other: in 1787 as farmer (Mills 1992).

504. Ashley, Nathaniel. Page 119. Occupation: farmer. Origin: Virginia. Family Status: wife and 7 children. Other: presenter of Nicolas Grenier.

505. Bailie, Juan. Page 119. Occupation: farmer. Origin: Maryland. Family Status: wife and 5 children. Other: lives on the Rio Nasau

506. Carter, Thomas. Page 119. Occupation: farmer. Origin: Virginia. Family Status: wife and 9 children.

507. Lofton, Juan. Page 119. Origin: Virginia. Family Status: wife and son. Other: in 1787, Protestant, farmer (Mills 1992).

508. Onell, Enrique. Page 119. Occupation: farmer. Origin: Virginia. Family Status: wife and 9 children. Other: in 1787 as Enrique O'Neil (Mills 1992).

509. Rain, Jose. Page 119. Occupation: farmer. Origin: Pennsylvania. Family Status: wife and 7 children. Other: in 1787 Mills (1992) indicates from Maryland.

510. Taylor, Roberto. Page 119. Occupation: farmer. Origin: Pennsylvania. Family Status: wife and 6 children. Other: fields of Bell

511. Brown, Pedro. Page 120. Occupation: ship's carpenter. Origin: Scotland. Family Status: wife and orphan girl.

512. Jones, Jacob. Page 120. Occupation: farmer. Origin: Virginia. Family Status: wife and 3 children.

513. Mayfield, Estevan. Page 120. Occupation: farmer. Origin: Virginia. Family Status: wife and a son. Other: As Stephen Mayfield, named as an arrested leader of robbers and murderers, in an Address of the 25th of January 1785 (Lockey 1949:471).

514. Milton, Miguel. Page 120. Occupation: not given. Origin: South Carolina. Family Status: single.

515. White, Jacobo. Page 120. Occupation: tailor. Origin: North Carolina. Family Status: wife and 2 children.

516. Godfrey, Guillermo. Page 121. Occupation: farmer. Origin: South Carolina. Family Status: family not living in the province. Other: He owns 5000 acres of land. As William Godfrey, he signed the Address of the Inhabitants of the River St. John of 25th of January 1785 (Lockey 1949:471).

517. Plummer, Daniel. Page 121. Occupation: farmer. Origin: Pennsylvania. Family Status: widower.

518. Russel, Guillermo. Page 121. Occupation: He manufactures money (*monedero*). Origin: Great Britain. Family Status: wife and 3 children. Other: left East Florida.

519. Smith, Levis. Page 121. Occupation: farmer. Origin: Pennsylvania. Family Status: wife and 4 children.

520. Welsh, Nicolas. Page 121. planter. Origin: New York. widower and 6 children. Other: owns 500 acres of land.

521. Crum, Solomon. Page 122. Occupation: building a schooner. Origin: South Carolina. Family Status: single with two brothers named Juan and Elijah. Other: left East Florida on the 10th of December.

522. Drury, Mills. Page 122. Occupation: farmer. Origin: South Carolina. Family Status: wife and 2 children.

523. Hendrick, Guillermo. Page 122. Occupation: ship builder. Origin: Pennsylvania. Family Status: wife and 5 children. Other: in 1787 Mills (1992) indicates farmer and millwright, from North Carolina.

524. Patrick, Daniel and Samuel. Page 122. Occupation: grocer (*tenero* in text = *tendero*), day laborer (*jornalero*).

525. Pritchard, Roberto. Page 122. Occupation: farmer. Origin: South Carolina. Family Status: wife. Other: owns 250 acres of land.

526. Truchet, Carlos. Page 122. Occupation: carpenter. Origin: South Carolina. Family Status: wife and 2 children. Other: left East Florida.

527. Esom, Juan. Page 123. Occupation: farmer. Origin: South Carolina. Family Status: wife and 4 children. Other: owns 250 acres of land.

528. Fincher, Jesse. Page 123. Occupation: farmer. Origin: South Carolina. Family Status: single. Other: owns 250 acres of land.

529. Legge, Eduardo. Page 123. Origin: England. Family Status: single.

530. Rogers, Gaspar. Page 123. Occupation: farmer. Origin: South Carolina. Family Status: widower and 5 children.

531. Simpson, Guillermo. Page 123. Occupation: farmer. Origin: North Carolina. Family Status: widower and son. Other: in 1787, carpenter and farmer, from England (Mills 1992).

532. Smylie, Juan. Page 123. Occupation: merchant. Origin: Scotland. Family Status: single.

533. Evinger, Gotlieb. Page 124. Occupation: farmer. Origin: Germany. Family Status: wife and 2 children. Other: left East Florida.

534. More, Jacobo. Page 124. Occupation: blacksmith. Origin: Georgia. Family Status: wife and 5 children. Other: There is a James Moore who, in 1784, is a private in the militia.

535. More, Hanah. Page 124. Occupation: farmer. Origin: Maryland. Family Status: widow and 2 children. Other: "Lives by Rio San Juan, 3 miles from the ranch of Master Fatio."

536. White, Enrique. Page 124. Occupation: ship's carpenter. Origin: Nova Scotia. Family Status: wife and 5 children.

537. Wiggins, Jose. Page 124. Occupation: Indian trader of the House of Panton. Origin: South Carolina. Other: He lives on the vacant ranch of Rolles. Family Status: wife and 3 children. Other: As Joe Wigengs, is one of the signers of Address of the Inhabitants of the River St. John of 25th of January 1785 (Lockey 1949:471).

538. Woltz, Gaspar. Page 124. Origin: South Carolina. Residence: "lives with the last named Evinger." Other: left East Florida.

539. Holman, Jose [in 1784 written Hohlinan]. Page 125. Occupation: sugar refiner, shoemaker. Origin: Germany. Family Status: wife. Other: in 1784 intends to remain in East Florida; private in the militia. A member of the company of Young.

540. Parr, Tomas. Page 125. Origin: England. Other: "He lives with the last named Ward."

541. Warantine, Guillermo. Page 125. Occupation: farmer. Origin: Virginia. Other: with his brother in law [*nuero* in text = *cuñado*] [Whitmore] intends to remain in East Florida.

542. Ward, Juan. Page 125. Occupation: agent of Don Dionis Rolles (resident of England) [who has] has 80,000 acres of land in this province. Origin: England. Family Status: single.

543. Whitmore, Roberto. Page 125. Occupation: farmer. Origin: North Carolina. Family Status: wife and son. Other: in 1784 intends to remain in East Florida. Other: in 1787, Protestant and from England (Mills 1992).

544. Blackwell, Esteban. Page 126. Occupation: farmer. Origin: Virginia. Family Status: single. Other: "He lives on the Rio San Juan in the house of Donaldo Cameron."

545. Blunt, Redden. Page 126. Occupation: farmer. Origin: North Carolina. Family Status: wife and 3 children. Other: He lives in New Smyrna.

546. Clements, James. Page 126. Occupation: mason. Origin: Ireland. Family Status: single. Other: "He lives in the house of Juan Flanagan Arnuro in San Augustine." James Clemmons was a private in the militia.

547. Dampier, Estevan. Page 126. Occupation: farmer. Origin: North Carolina. Family Status: wife. Other: He lives in New Smyrna.

548. NAME MISSING. Page 126. Occupation: baker. Family Status: wife.

549. Tomson, Jacobo. Page 126. Occupation: carpenter. Origin: Ireland. Family Status: single. Other: "He lives on the ranch of Mr. Bannes."

550. Williams, Wilson. Page 126. Occupation: farmer. Origin: North Carolina. Family Status: wife and son. Other: a private in

the militia. As Wilson Williams, he signed the "Address" of the River St. John of 25th of January 1785 (Lockey 1949:471).

551. Andrews, Samuel. Page 127. Occupation: planter. Origin: North Carolina. Family Status: wife and 4 children. Also an unmarried brother called Juan. Other: was a private in the militia.

552. Davis, Thomas. Page 127. Occupation: bugler (*clarin*). Origin: Virginia. Family Status: single.

553. Doharty, Jacobo. Page 127. Occupation: farmer. Origin: Virginia. Family Status: single.

554. Hermans, Pedro. Page 127. Occupation: farmer. Origin: Georgia. Family Status: single. Also his brothers Guillermo and Thomas. They all live with their mother.

555. Johnston, Guillermo. Page 127. Occupation: farmer. Origin: Virginia. Family Status: wife and son. Other: William Johnston signed the "Address" of June 6, 1783 (Lockey 1949:115).

556. Macleod, Jacobo. Page 127. Occupation: farmer. Origin: Georgia. Family Status: single. Has a sister.

557. Morpus, Riccardo. Page 127. Occupation: farmer. Origin: Virginia. Family Status: wife and son.

558. Westley, Jacobo. Page 127. Occupation: farmer. Origin: England. Family Status: single. Other: "He lives on the Rio San Juan near Mr. Bailye."

559. Cabler, Adan. Page 128. Occupation: farmer. Origin: Germany. Family Status: wife and son.

560. Coue [*or* Cobe *or* Cove], Micajah. Page 128. Occupation: sailor. Origin: Virginia. Family Status: widower.

561. Cuitt, Amos. Page 128. Occupation: carpenter. Origin: Virginia. Family Status: wife and son.

562. Keller, Juan. Page 128. Occupation: farmer. Origin: South Carolina. Family Status: single. Other: left East Florida.

563. King, Sebastian. Page 128. Occupation: carpenter. Origin: England. Family Status: family left.

564. Miller, Ricardo. Page 128. Occupation: farmer. Origin: England. Family Status: wife and son.

565. Noland, Jacobo. Page 128. Origin: Virginia.

566. Brown, Juan. Page 129. Occupation: farmer. Origin: Pennsylvania. Family Status: single. Other: John Brown is one of the signers of an "Address of the Principal Inhabitants to Governor Tonyn" of June 6, 1783 (Lockey 1949:115).

567. Phillips, Juan. Page 129. Occupation: farmer. Origin: North Carolina. Family Status: single.

568. Sally, Enrique. Page 129. Origin: South Carolina. Family Status: wife.

569. Warner, Pedro. Page 129. Occupation: farmer. Origin: Germany. Family Status: family left. Other: left East Florida.

570. White, Estevan. Page 129. Occupation: shopkeeper. Origin: Ireland. Family Status: wife and son.

571. Whiteman, Jacobo. Page 129. Occupation: blacksmith. Origin: South Carolina. Family Status: single.

572. Phillips, Daniel. Page 129.-130 Occupation: farmer. Origin: Georgia. Family Status: wife and 3 children in Carolina and a niece and a girl servant at his house in East Florida..

573. Drennen, David. Page 130. Occupation: farmer. Origin: Pennsylvania. Family Status: wife and 3 children. Other: lives on the island of Malta.

574. Lowry, Luis. Page 130. Occupation: farmer. Origin: Virginia. Family Status: single.

575. Reddy, Guillermo. Page 130. Occupation: fisherman. Origin: United States. Family Status: wife. Other: owns 350 acres of land.

576. Roke, Samuel. Page 130. Occupation: farmer. Origin: South Carolina. Family Status: single. Other: left East Florida.

577. Shocker, Gaspar. Page 130. Occupation: farmer. Origin: South Carolina. Family Status: single.

578. Ashbraner, Felipe. Page 131. Occupation: weaver. Origin: Pennsylvania. Family Status: single.

579. Ashworth, Arturo. Page 131. Occupation: soldier. Origin: North Carolina. Family Status: single.

580. Colliday, Jacob. Page 131. Occupation: wheelwright (*carpenter de ruedas*) Origin: Philadelphia [Pennsylvania]. Family Status: wife, 5 children, and sister in law..

581. Downer, Moises. Page 131. Occupation: farmer. Origin: South Carolina. Family Status: wife.

582. Elsberry Peters, Solomon. Page 131. Recorded "in her name and in the name of her husband who is absent in Georgia." Occupation: farmer. Origin: Virginia. Family Status: 2 children.

583. Howard, Abrahan. Page 131. Occupation: farmer. Origin: Virginia. Family Status: single.

584. Neal, Thomas. Page 131. Origin: North Carolina. Other: page is not torn, entry is incomplete but is not continued on the next page.

585. Touchstone, Esteban. Page 131. Occupation: carpenter. Origin: North Carolina. Family Status: single.

586. Austin, David. Page 132. Occupation: sailor. Origin: England. Family Status: single. Other: As David Auston, signed the Address ... of 25th of January 1785 (Lockey 1949:471).

587. Harris, Guillermo. Page 132. Occupation: farmer. Origin: Georgia. Family Status: wife and 4 children.

588. Mills, Josef. Page 132. Occupation: farmer. Origin: Maryland?. Family Status: wife. Other: Lives with his father Samuel in the locality called "Cedar Point."

589. Spicer, Christopher. Page 132. Occupation: planter. Origin: Maryland. Family Status: wife, 2 children and sister in law.

590. Smith, Carlos. Pages 132-133. Occupation: farmer. Origin: Ireland. Other: agent for Field Marshal Tonyn. One plantation of Tonyn has a white overseer called Thomas Mall and other, the white overseer Tomathon MacCullch.

591. Bouden, Ysac. Page 133. Occupation: farmer. Origin: Maryland. Family Status: wife and 8 children. Other: in 1784 intends to remain in East Florida. In 1787 as Issack Bowden (Mills 1992).

592. Guilbert, Roberto [spelt Gilbert in 1784]. Page 133. Occupation: builder of boats and canoes, farmer. Origin: North Carolina. Family Status: wife and 6 children. "He has a father of close to 100 years old who is incapable of moving." Other: "He could not respond directly, but instead through Mr. Bouden, because of illness."

593. Hall, Juan. Page 133. Occupation: farmer. Origin: Virginia. Family Status: wife and 2 children.

594. Ledford, Federico. Page 133. Occupation: farmer. Origin: North Carolina. Family Status: wife and 2 children. Other: " He lives 4 miles from the interpreter Briart." In 1784 he intended to remain in East Florida.

595. Maliard, Daniel. Page 133. Occupation: carpenter. Origin: Virginia. Family Status: wife and 3 children. Other: "He lives with the previously mentioned Hall."

596. Flake, Juan. Page 134. Occupation: farmer. Origin: Virginia. Family Status: single. Other: "He lives with Samuel Holaway." left East Florida.

597. Holaway, Samuel. Page 134. Occupation: farmer. Origin: Pennsylvania. Family Status: "His wife and son went away."

598. Hulint, Thomas. Page 134. Occupation: farmer. Origin: North Carolina. Family Status: single. Other: "He lives with Mr. Derry."

599. Martin, Mathews. Page 134. Occupation: farmer. Origin: North Carolina. Family Status: single. Other: "He lives with Mr. Ashworth."

600. Murphy, Thomas. Page 134. Occupation: farmer. Origin: Pennsylvania. Family Status: single.

601. Stafford, Roberto. Page 134. Occupation: farmer. Origin: England. Family Status: single. Other: foreman on a ranch of Mr. Wilkinson.

602. Stubbs, Wade. Page 134. Occupation: farmer. Origin: England. Family Status: single. Other: He owns 1,400 acres of land.

603. Tustin, Tomas. Page 134. Occupation: carpenter. Origin: Pennsylvania. Family Status: wife and 4 children.

604. Gibson, Gideon. Pages 134-135. Occupation: farmer. Origin: South Carolina. Family Status: single. Other: He supports his mother and a sister. In 1784 he intends to remain in East Florida.

605. Macdonald, Alexandro. Page 135. Occupation: farmer. Origin: Scotland. Family Status: widower and children.

606. Smith, Guillermo. Page 135. Occupation: silversmith. Origin: North Carolina. Family Status: wife and son.

607. Travis, Aaron. Page 135. Occupation: farmer. Origin: South Carolina. Family Status: single. Lives with 2 brothers and a widowed sister who has a son. Other: in 1787 as Aaron Travies (Ball 1992).

608. Williams, Samuel. Page 135. Origin: North Carolina. Family Status: widower and son. Other: French overseer Ferrio. As Samuel Williams, is one of the signers of Address of the Inhabitants of the River St. John of 25th of January 1785 (Lockey 1949:471).

609. Gray, Archibaldo. Pages 135-136. Occupation: ship's carpenter. Origin: Scotland. Family Status: wife. Other: "He lived near the warehouse of Mr. Corbert on Amalia island." He left East Florida.

610. Linder, Juan [Junior]. Page 136. Occupation: farmer. Origin: South Carolina. Family Status: wife and 2 children. Other: "He lives in a house given to Francisco Sanches." He left on the 26th of October with his family for Pensacola. Identified by Tanner (1989:43) as a "member of McGirt gang hustled out of the province in November by an escort of Spanish dragoons."

611. Philips, Jorje. Page 136. Occupation: farmer. Origin: Virginia Family Status: wife. Other: "His residence was previously occupied by Juan Guillermo." Other: He left via West Florida for New Orleans.

612. Safold, Ysham. Page 136. Occupation: watchmaker, silversmith, ship's carpenter and builder of wind and water mills. Origin: Virginia. Family Status: wife and 2 children.

613. MacGirit, Jacobo. Pages 136-137. Occupation: farmer Origin: Carolina. Family Status: wife and 2 children. Other: "He lives on the vacant ranch of Senor Rolles." He intended, in 1784 to leave via West Florida for New Orleans. In 1786, identified as Jayme MacGirt, Lutheran, age 50 (Mills 1992). He was identified by Tanner (1989:43) as James McGirt, a member of the McGirt gang that "settled down in Saint Augustine and joined respectable society."

614. Bailie, Alexandro. Page 137. Occupation: farmer. Origin: Scotland. Family Status: single.

615. Bradley, Josef. Page 137. Occupation: day laborer (*jornalero*) in 1784. Origin: South Carolina. Family Status: single. Other: "He lives in the house of Daniel MacGirit." In 1784 he intended to remain in East Florida.

616. Cargan, Daniel. Page 137. Occupation: farmer. Origin: Virginia. Family Status: single. Other: "He lives in the house of Estevan Mayfield." In 1784 intended to move to Louisiana.

617. Forester, Alexandro. Page 137. Occupation: lawyer. Origin: South Carolina. Family Status: single.

618. Whaley, Guillermo. Page 137. Occupation: day laborer (jornalero). Origin: South Carolina. Family Status: unmarried. Other: "He lives in the house of Mr. Cann." He intends to leave via West Florida for New Orleans.

619. Brown, Hugo. Page 138. Occupation: farmer. Origin: Virginia. Family Status: wife and 4 children. Other: sergent in the militia.

620. Files, Estevan. Page 138. Occupation: shopkeeper. Origin: England. Family Status: single.

621. Henis, Juan. Page 138. Occupation: farmer. Origin: Maryland. Family Status: wife and 3 children. Other: in 1784 intends to remain in East Florida.

622. MacCormick, Jose. Page 138. Occupation: farmer. Origin: Pennsylvania. Family Status: wife and 2 children. Other: private in the militia.

623. Proctor, Felipe. Page 138. Occupation: farmer. Origin: Ireland. Family Status: wife. Other: "He lives in the same house as MacCormick, Jose. He is a private in the militia.

624. Smith, Benjamin. Page 138. Occupation: shopkeeper for dry goods. Origin: South Carolina. Family Status: single.

624. Smith, Benjamin. Page 138. Occupation: shopkeeper for dry goods. Origin: South Carolina. Family Status: single.

625. Bogian, Guillermo. Page 138.-139. Occupation: farmer. Origin: South Carolina. Family Status: wife. Other: in 1787 given as Guillermo Bogin (Mills 1992).

626. Crawford, Juan. Page 139. Occupation: farmer. Origin: Pennsylvania. Family Status: wife and nephew called Juan Campbee. Other: As John Crafford was a private in the militia. He has a ranch of 200 acres of land. As John Campbell, his nephew, was a private in the militia.

627. Fleuret, Francisco. Page 139. Occupation: shoemaker. Origin: American. Family Status: wife and 4 children. Other: intends to go to Louisiana.

628. Mitchell, Guillermo. Page 139. Occupation: farmer. Origin: South Carolina. Other: private in the militia. As William Mitchell, one of the signers of Address of the Inhabitants of the River St. John of 25th of January 1785 (Lockey 1949:471).

629. Murphy, Juan. Page 139. Occupation: physician. Origin: Ireland. Family Status: widower, son, grandson.

630. Oaets, Tamer. Page 139. Origin: Georgia. Family Status: son.

631. Pengree, Guillermo. Page 139. Occupation: planter. Origin: American. Family Status: wife and 2 children. Other: in 1787, farmer, English (Mills 1992).

632. Sterling, Francisco. Page 139. Occupation: farmer. Origin: Pennsylvania. Other: Listed as private Francis Sterling in the militia.

633. Braker, Joraje. Page 140. Origin: Germany. Family Status: wife and 3 children. Other: As George Brakor, is one of the signers of Address of the Inhabitants of the River St. John of 25th of January 1785 (Lockey 1949:471). He lives in Potberg.

634. Chapman, Guillermo. Page 140. Occupation: farmer. Origin: South Carolina. Family Status: single.

635. Denny, Samuel. Page 140. Occupation: farmer. Origin: Virginia. Family Status: wife and son.

636. Hopkins, Juan. Page 140. Occupation: master of ship. Origin: England. Family Status: wife and 2 children.

637. Smith, Enrique. Page 140. Occupation: farmer. Origin: South Carolina.

638. Wordin, Thomas. Page 140. Occupation: tanner, shoemaker, carpenter and farmer. Origin: Virginia. Family Status: wife and 4 children.

639. Brackstone, Guillermo. Page 141. Origin: England.

640. Castlake, Samuel. Page 141. Occupation: surgeon. Origin: England. Family Status: single.

641. King, Ricardo. Page 141. Origin: England. Family Status: widower, son, sister in law.

642. MacDermott, Juan. Page 141. Occupation: mercantile. Origin: Ireland. Family Status: single.

643. MacDonald, Reynaldo. Page 141. Occupation: farmer. Origin: Scotland. Family Status: wife and 4 children. Other: 150 acres of land.

644. MacDonell, Alexandro. Page 141. Occupation: mercantile. Origin: Scotland. Family Status: single. Other: As A. Macdonell, is one of the signers of Address of the Inhabitants of the River St. John of 25th of January 1785 (Lockey 1949:471). In 1786, Catholic, farmer, age 26 (Mills 1992).

645. MacDonell, Randolfo. Page 141. Occupation: farmer. Origin: Scotland. Family Status: single. Other: As Randolph Macdonell, is one of the signers of Address of the Inhabitants of the River St. John of 25th of January 1785 (Lockey 1949:471). In 1786, Catholic, age 45 (Mills 1992).

646. Buckingham, Clias. Pages 141-142. Occupation: carpenter and chairmaker. Origin: England. Family Status: single.

647. Hopton, Abner. Page 142. Occupation: carpenter. Origin: Pennsylvania. Family Status: single. Other: "He works on the ranch of Mr. Pengree." He intends to move to West Florida.

648. Hungerpeler, Jacobo. Page 142. Occupation: farmer. Origin: South Carolina. Other: left East Florida.

649. Johnston, Juan. Page 142. Occupation: farmer. Origin: Georgia. Family Status: wife and 4 children. Other: "He lives on the vacant ranch of Dabes." John Johnston is one of the signers of an "Address of the Principal Inhabitants to Governor Tonyn" of June 6, 1783 (Lockey 1949:115).

650. Lysett, Patricio. Page 142. Occupation: "vacant" in 1784. Origin: Ireland. Family Status: wife and 4 children.

651. Smith, Jacobo. Page 142. Occupation: baker. Origin: Virginia. Family Status: single. Other: in 1784 intends to remain in East Florida. Other: James Smith is one of the signers of an "Address of the Principal Inhabitants to Governor Tonyn" of June 6, 1783 (Lockey 1949:115).

652. Snell, Enrique. Page 142. Occupation: farmer. Origin: South Carolina.

653. Stoughtenmire, Jorje. Page 142. Occupation: farmer. Origin: Germany.

654. Whitman, Guillermo. Page 142. Occupation: farmer. Origin: South Carolina. Family Status: single.

655. Fridig, David. [Friday in 1784]. Page 143. Occupation: farmer in 1784 Origin: South Carolina. Family Status: wife and 7 children. Other: left East Florida.

656. Ingram, Guillermo. Page 143. Origin: England. Family Status: wife and 3 children. Other: left East Florida.

657. Johnson, Jorge. Page 143. Occupation: farmer. Origin: North Carolina. Family Status: wife and 2 children.

658. Keller, Gaspar. Page 143. Occupation: farmer. Origin: Germany. Family Status: single. Other: left East Florida.

659. Mulkey, Juan. Page 143. Occupation: farmer. Origin: North Carolina. Family Status: single.

660. Pace, David. Page 143. Occupation: farmer. Origin: Georgia. Family Status: wife and 2 children.

661, Poyner, Josef. Page 143. Occupation: tax assessor ? (*contade tasamani*). Origin: North Carolina. Family Status: single.

662. Shireman, Felipe. Page 143. Occupation: blacksmith. Origin: Germany. Family Status: single.

663. Sloan, Jacobo. Page 143. Occupation: farmer. Origin: Pennsylvania. Family Status: single.

664. Wise, Juan. Page 143. Occupation: farmer. Origin: Germany. Family Status: wife and 3 children.

665. Elleby, Ysham. Pages 143-144. Occupation: farmer. Origin: South Carolina. Family Status: single.

666. Bunkley, Britain. Page 144. Occupation: farmer. Origin: Virginia. Family Status: wife and 3 children.

667. Conway, Carlos. Page 144. Occupation: farmer. Origin: Virginia. Family Status: wife and 4 children. Other: "lives with his

brother Guillermo Conway." He intends to go via West Florida to the Mississippi.

668. Conway, Guillermo. Page 144. Occupation: farmer. Origin: Virginia. Family Status: wife and son.

669. Keary [or Leary], Jesse. Page 144. Occupation: farmer. Origin: Pennsylvania. Family Status: wife, son and brother.

670. MacLeod, Donald. Page 144. Occupation: farmer. Origin: Georgia. Family Status: wife. Other: intends to leave East Florida.

671. Macoy, Jacobo. Page 144. Occupation: sailor. Origin: "from the Sea." Family Status: single. Other: intends to return to the Ocean.

672. Spalding, Ysham. Page 144. Occupation: carpenter. Origin: Virginia. Family Status: wife and son. Other: has 150 acres and land on the Matanzas river.

673. Clasworthy, Jacobo. Page 145. Occupation: planter. Origin: South Carolina. Family Status: wife and son.

674. Cole, Juana. Page 145. Origin: Georgia. Family Status: widow and son.

675. Douglas, Maria, Page 145. Origin: South Carolina. Family Status: widow and 4 children.

676. Felts, Susana, Page 145. Occupation: "vacant" in 1784. Origin: South Carolina. Family Status: widow with a baby.

677. Hallums, Sara, Page 145. Origin: South Carolina. Family Status: widow and 4 children, Other: in 1787 as Sara Hall (Mills 1992).

678. Peirgler, Enrrique, Page 145. Origin: Germany. Family Status: wife and 2 children.

679. Quenaud, Juan Pedro, Page 145. Occupation: gardener. Origin: Geneva [Switzerland]. Family Status: wife and 2 children.

Other: in 1784 intends to stay in East Florida.

680. Sullivan, Daniel. Page 145. Occupation: tailor. Origin: Ireland. Family Status: single.

681. Tallack, Jorje. Page 145. Occupation: carpenter. Origin: England. Family Status: wife and son. Other: left East Florida.

682. Blackman, Wood. Page 146. Occupation: farmer. Origin: Virginia. Family Status: wife and son.

683. Clarke, Thomas. Page 146. Occupation: farmer. Origin: Virginia. Family Status: single.

684. Crudi, Hermano. Page 146. Occupation: farmer. Origin: Germany. Family Status: wife.

685. Fletcher, Josiah. Page 146. Occupation: farmer. Family Status: single.

686. Fregin, Jorje. Page 146. Occupation: farmer. Origin: North Carolina. Family Status: single.

687. Steigler, Juan. Page 146. Occupation: farmer. Origin: South Carolina. Family Status: wife and son.

688. Thorp, Allen. Page 146. Occupation: farmer. Origin: Virginia. Family Status: wife. Other: "lives with the previous mentioned Blackman."

689. Hemdricks, Juan. Page 147. Origin: North Carolina. Family Status: wife and 2 children.

690. Hunter, Roberto. Page 147. Occupation: pilot for a ship. Origin: England. Family Status: wife and son.

691. Splaun, Guillermo. Page 147. Occupation: farmer. Origin: South Carolina. Family Status: single. Other: "lives with the last named Hemdricks."

692. Swanson, David. Page 147. Occupation: blacksmith. Origin: Scotland. Family Status: 3 children and no wife.

693. Whaly, Juan. Page 147. Occupation: farmer. Origin: South Carolina. Family Status: single.

694. Wimbesley, Abraham. Page 147. Occupation: carpenter and farmer. Origin: North Carolina. Family Status: single.

695. Wornal, Miguel. Page 147. Occupation: farmer. Origin: Pennsylvania. Family Status: wife and 3 children.

696. Arons, Jorje. Page 163. Occupation: farmer. Alsace France. Family Status: wife and son. Other: in 1784 intends to stay in East Florida.

697. Comebest, Simon. Page 163. Occupation: carpenter. Origin: Virginia. Family Status: single.

698. Crier, Morgan. Page 163. Occupation: farmer. Origin: South Carolina. Family Status: wife and son.

699. How, Nathaniel. Page 163. Occupation: "the sea." Origin: New York. Family Status: single. Other: "lives on the ranch of Mr. Egan."

700. Young, Juan. Page 163. Occupation: farmer. Origin: Maryland. Family Status: wife. Other: sergent in the militia.

701. Young, Samuel. Page 163. Occupation: farmer. Origin: Maryland. Family Status: single.

702. Youngblood, Jese. Page 163. Origin: South Carolina. Family Status: single.

703. Bynum, Jacobo. Page 164. Occupation: farmer. Origin: North Carolina. Family Status: wife and 4 children.

704. Dell, Phelip. Page 164. Occupation: farmer. Origin: Virginia. Family Status: single.

705. Egger, Juan. Page 164. Occupation: farmer. Origin: Ireland. Family Status: wife.

706. Griffith, Cornelio. Page 164. Occupation: farmer. Origin: South Carolina. Family Status: wife and son. In 1787, joiner, Protestant (Mills 1992).

707. Peters, Solomon. Page 164. Occupation: farmer. Origin: Virginia. Family Status: wife and 3 children.

708. Stephason, Diego. Page 164. Occupation: farmer. Origin: Pennsylvania. Family Status: single. Other: "He lives with Don Enrique Onell."

709. Williams, Juan. Page 164. Occupation: iron founder Origin: Pennsylvania. Family Status: wife and 2 children..

710. Yewbank, Estevan. Page 164. Occupation: carpenter. Origin: Virginia. Family Status: wife and 6 children.

711. Chapel, Jacobo. Page 165. Occupation: farmer. Origin: South Carolina. Family Status: single. Other: "He lives near Major Neely." "He has a black with Colonel Young."

712. Karrel, Jacobo. Page 165. Occupation: farmer. Origin: South Carolina. Family Status: wife.

713. Powell, Guillermo. Page 165. Occupation: farmer. Origin: South Carolina. Family Status: wife and 4 children.

714. Shoemaker, Daniel. Page 165. Occupation: farmer. Origin: Virginia. Family Status: wife and 2 children.

Appendix 1. Militia on the 6th of August 1784.[28]

Ashley, William	Sergeant
Berry, Michael	private
Bishop, Elijah	private
Bishop, William	private
Bolton, Robert	private
Bryant, Hawkins	private
Drew, William	private
Ebner, Jacob	private
Fitch, Andrews	private
Fort, Drury	Sergeant
French, Robert	private
Goldsby, Thomas	private
Goodbread, Philip	private
Gray, Samuel	Lieutenant
Hall, Nathaniel	private
Hutson, Rush	private
Jenkins, Richard	private
King, Solomon	private
Lucas, William	Lieutenant
Penticost, Hartivel	private
Prescot, Felse	private
Proctor, Edward	private
Scott, John	private
Siblet, William	private
Sisley, Martin	private
Smith, Ezekiel	private
Summerlin, Peter	private
Tate, Jeremiah	private
Tate, William	private
Williams, William	private

---

[28]Militia members mentioned in the "List of all English residents at the change of Flag in 1784" are not listed here. Drury Fort, John Scot, William Bishop, Joseph Summerlin, Phillip Proctor, Robert Bolton, Phillip Goodbread and Solomon King are signers of Address of the Inhabitants of the River St. John of 25th of January 1785 (Lockey 1949:471).

Appendix 2. Residents on

a Street in Saint Augustine

CARLOTA STREET

Armstrong, Fleetwood
Barnes, Jorge
Boak, Don Thomas
Burgess, Thomas
Christie, Maria
Clarke, Dona Honoria
Curtis, Guillermo
Cuthbert, Jacobo
Delegall, Sara
Ficher, Juan
Flemming, Don Jorje
Gomila, Jose
Heley, Don Juan
Hombard, Bernardo
Johnson, Don Juan
Johnson, Guillermo
Love, Juan
MacFarlan, Juan
Moises, David
More, Dorotea
Newberry, Enrique
Orr, Don Thomas
Pons, Jose
Reed, Roberto
Reynolds, Juan
Rigby, Thomas
Scotland, Jacobo
Sheriff, Don Pedro
Simpson, Thomas
Slater, Guillermo

Stage, Federico
Storr, Don Juan
Taylor, Jacobo
Wales, Jacobo

and Two Islands on the
North East Coast

TALBOT ISLAND

Chapman, Guillermo
Dell, Phelip
Elsberry Peters, Solomon
Peters, Solomon
Simpson, Guillermo
Spicer, Christopher
Touchstone, Esteban
Whitmore, Roberto
Young, Alexandro

AMALIA ISLAND

Bynum, Jacobo
Egger, Juan
Gray, Archibaldo
Karrel, Jacobo
Safold, Ysham
Shoemaker, Daniel
Williams, Juan
Yewbank, Estevan
Young, Juan
Young, Samuel
Youngblood, Jese

Appendix 3. Other Names mentioned in associated documents

These are mostly British subjects who filed a petition requesting permission to stay in East Florida longer than the permitted time in order to allow them to find buyers for their property. An abstract of these petitions, and the verdict of the Spanish authorities, is included on pages 169-172 of this volume.

Meter, Don Guillermo	169	beginning with the 19th of the present month of March a 3 month extension is granted
Moore, Thomas	169	together with his mother, 2 months of requested extension is granted
Mowbray, Don Juan[29]	169	11th of March [left]
Jmant, Juan	170	[extensions]
Merlin, Eduardo	170	[extensions]
Warner, Ysabel	170	[extensions]
Ball, Colonel Don Elias[30]	171	forbid the sale [of his property]
Henderson, Barbara	172	[extensions]
Muhie, Carlos	172	[extensions]

---

[29]John Mowbray is one of the signers of an "Address of the Principal Inhabitants to Governor Tonyn" of June 6, 1783 (Lockey 1949:115).

[30]Elias Ball is one of the signers of an "Address of the Principal Inhabitants to Governor Tonyn" of June 6, 1783 (Lockey 1949:115).

Appendix 4. October 1784 Census

Saint Augustine of Florida. 20th of October of 1784. The Governor of the garrison of Florida sends to Your Excellency the comprehensive census, of the families and of their decisions of the Catholic subjects and Britons who reside here, in virtue of the order published on the previous 14th of July.

Excellency, My Dear Sir:

In my letter of the previous 16th of July, I communicated to Your Excellency the edict proclaimed on the 14th of the same month in consequence of I prepared a comprehensive Census of all the British inhabitants, including with their names, the number of families, of slaves, of land holdings, of livestock, residences, occupation, religion of each head of family, of those that desire to remain or uncertain with regard to remaining under the dominion of His Majesty.

The names and occupations of the Minorcans were not collected being that these are considered the natural vassals of His Majesty as noted in the petition submitted previously on the 16th [?] of July. In general these Minorcans are all a working people, highborn as well as low. Although raised among the English, they have kept their Catholic religion and use of the mother language. Some are merchants, others are farmers, others fish. Among them are very few with craft specialization's. Among the merchants, their capital goes from a thousand to eight thousand pesos. And some of these are owners of sloops and schooners. Most of them plant crops in a field close to the city, few or none own their own land. They rent four or five adjacent [fields] for sowing maize and some vegetables. With respect to orders of Your Excellency from His Majesty, upon the expiration of the indicated 18 months established by the treaty, those lands not sold by the [departing] British are available for the Royal Service and it would be an act of royal mercy to order divided portions of the said lands among these people in proportion to the size of each family.

I have at the same time requested that Your Excellency communicate the Royal Will with regard to the British Apostolic Roman Catholics, those desiring to convert to the holy faith and those others who, without informing us of their religion, desire to remain or are undecided upon remaining. Also I ask Your Excellency to advise me of the intention of His Majesty relative to those punishments permitted by article 5 of the mentioned treaty. The inhabitants of the city are, in general, quiet and peaceful. Those men with a bad reputation are well known and not discussed in my correspondence with the former English Governor.

They all live outside of the City, most being Americans who having ferociously supported the royal party would never would be permitted to return to the United States. Seven, who Field Marshal Tonyn has not claimed for his own, returned to their original occupations. The word of the definitive treaty [is] to the taste of the hidden villains. And with unanimity they continue to clutch the pardon offered with my authority... [to avoid trouble] rather than in love of Justice for the known criminals. The state of the country gives freedom to many bad subjects, who are careful to be compliant in order not to give a pretext [for expulsion]. It seems they don't want anything more than to be allowed to work on the plantings, and [this is] especially [true] for the representative of the Lord Tonyn and four others who worked for him. Following the instructions of Your Excellency I remain compliant , except when confronted with an actual crime. Of these turbulent men, in general none of them want war. I am sure neither before nor after the 18 months expire nor will they ever retire to British Domains.

God Guard Your Excellency and His Majesty for many needed happy years. Florida, 20th of October 1784.

[Vicente Manuel de Zespedes, Governor]

name	Position	Origin	Fam. Size	Intentions
Brid, Juan[31]	carpenter	American		Louisiana
Carney, Arturo	trader	American	1	uncertain
Cheny, Beley[32]	planter	American	4	Louisiana
Collins, Guillermo[33]	planter	American	5	Louisiana
David, Guillermo	farmer	American		remain
Heineman, Barbara[34]	farmer	Germany	8	remain
Laws, Juan	farmer	Ireland		uncertain
Linham, Guillermo	carpenter	American	7	remain
Miller, Samuel	baker	American	6	remain
Moor, Jacobo	farmer	Ireland	2	remain
Pedro, Guillermo	farmer	American	2	remain
Pedro, Thomas	farmer	American		remain
Powell, Jorfe Henderson	planter	England	2	remain
Robins, Josef	farmer	American	1	Louisiana
Tompson, Jorje	farmer	Scotland	3	uncertain
Tuday, Daniel	farmer	American	1	Louisiana
Wright, Thomas	cooper	Ireland	3	uncertain

---

[31] Lived on or near the Rio San Juan. This is also true for Guillermo Pedro, Thomas Pedro, Jorje Tompson, and Thomas Wright.

[32] Lived on or near the Rio Nasaw. Belay Cheney, native of North Carolina, in a statement of five Americans who are disturbing the peace of the country of 15th of July 1784, wishes to avail himself of Spanish protection and settle in Louisiana. He has a wife, two children, eight slaves and two horses (Lockey 1949:236).

[33] William Collins, a native of South Carolina, in a statement of five Americans who are disturbing the peace of the country of 15th of July 1784, wishes to avail himself of Spanish protection and settle in Louisiana. He is a widower, with four children, and four slaves (Lockey 1949:236).

[34] Lived on or near the Rio del Norte.

Appendix 5. "Blacks found without an owner who have been permitted to be rented in the name of the American who has them."

1. John James. Black who fled from South Carolina to claim protection who is clearly not of this country and declared of his own free will his willingness to work for the Minorquin Pedro Bedell [Pere Vedell, Rasico 1990: 169] who remains jailed by the government because of a robbery made previously of a Spaniard.

2. Robin Negro. Left with the English from the site of Charleston with the cavalry of Colonel Cruden in the time of the war... to Florida where he served a soldier of the company of Captain Don Alexander Vchuaart...

3. Ham Negro. Robbed from an American vassal called Carlos Eliot of Charleston and taken to this province by a British vassal named Tarberry...

4. Saunders Negro. He was slave in Carolina of an American vassal named Edward Harleston from whom he escaped and ... at the orders of Count Cornwallis came after the evacuation of Charleston [where] he is living with the Mallorquín Pedro Bedell...

5. Mary or María Negra. wife of the previous. Came with him from Carolina and went with him to this place... living with the Mallorquín Pedro Bedell.

6. Sandy Negro was a slave in South Carolina of Juan Werin from whom he was taken by a sergeant of the English army who sold him in Savannah to a white Englishman whose name he didn't know but knowing that he had business among the Indians for a few days, returned to Charleston where he embarked on the schooner of Captain Wallace and came to this...

7. Negro Jo was a slave of Thomas Bee in South Carolina from whom he fled when the English besieged Charleston... he lives with the Minorquin Juan Andreu (from Mercadal, Minorca, farmer; Rasico 1990:158).

8. John Negro. He was a slave of Colonel Du Vaux who was sold to a Frenchman in New York. When his [owner] died the black escaped on board a Brig called La Polly... he works ... with the Minorquin Francisco de Borgo.

9. Primus Negro. He had fled from his master Mr. Pastel inhabitant of South Carolina ... he desires to live with Pedro de Cala.

10. Joe Negro says he had fled from Georgia the past year... from his master Captain Guna and passed to this province where he was put to work with the poor Englishman called Denny ...

11. Katy Negro with her child were freed by the ... signature of Colonel Brown.

12. Cyrus or Cyro Negro. It is said that this slave fled from Mr. Gerald of Georgia and ... and to this province with Colonel Brown.. placed under the Spaniard Mateo Acosta Guadarrama.

13. Sharper Negro with his wife Nancy, were recognized as free by the signature of General MacArthur.

14. The mulatto Juan Gray[35] had presented sworn documents supporting his liberty.

15. Pedro and Maria, Negro and Negra, say them came from Charleston perhaps three years ago [with] a captain of regiment number 60, who sold them to William Kane from whom they were robbed by Samuel Moor who took was taking them to an Indian nation but they escaped enroute and came to this place where.. they voluntarily serve the Minorquin Jose Pons.... They express the [desire to] live with Pedro de Cala.

16. Carlos Negro came from America in the years of the last war. Belonging to the councilor Lu Drayton, he saw Charleston but

---

[35]This may be the same John Gray who is one of the signers of Address of the Inhabitants of the River St. John of 25th of January 1785 (Lockey 1949:471).

departed in the English evacuation and remained free as a consequence.... He freely works for Don Carlos Howard.

17. Robin from the same master and with the same circumstances as the previous and has been placed to serve Don Fernando Arredondo.

18. Sam belonged in South Carolina to a Mr. Henry Alexander, British vassal and captain de Militia in the last war, who is married with the widow Bodd, original owner of Sam, hearing that he wanted to sell him, he escaped and came with Major Williams to this province in company of another black Hector and his wife ... and at the time of evacuation of the province of the said major, the said Sam fled from him to live as free with Don Francisco Felipe Fatio.

19. Hector and Rein, belonged to Diego Devaux[36] in Savannah and had served in the British army against the Americans ... thrust into the company of the previously mentioned Major Williams they came to this Florida where he and his wife live as free... he lives with his wife as free with Don Francisco Phelipe Fatio

20. William Williams, subject of Great Britain, lived previously in this province.. he said that in the month of December 1784, four blacks of his property, and of his brother, called Sam, Hector, Cesar and Reina fled from his service at the moment he was to leave the said province, following the treaty of peace of the two monarchs... and in a short time were found in the Plantation of Don Francisco Felipe Fatio... 5 March 1788.

---

[36]Jacob Deveaux is one of the signers of a "Memorial and Petition of the Inhabitants of East Florida" of September 11, 1783 (Lockey 1949:158).

Appendix 6. Government in British East Florida

List of British Governors (based on data in Schafer 1983)

(1) Captain John Hedges, July 1763

(2) Major Francis Ogilvie, August 1763- August 1764

(3) Colonel James Grant
arrival on August 29, 1764
formally assumed position on October 31, 1764
left for England on May 1771,
resigned governorship in April 1773

(4) Lieutenant Governor John Moultrie, May 1771-March 1774

(5) Lieutenant Colonel[37] ("Field Marshall") Patrick Tonyn,
Arrival of Tonyn, March 1774
Arrival of the Spanish governor, June 27 1784
British officials move to the St. Mary's River, June 1, 1785
Departure of Tonyn for England, November 1785

Commons House of Assembly members in 1781 (Mowat 1964:164)

Robert Payne	John Martin
John Ross	Thomas Ross
Stephen Egan	Philip Moore
George Kemp	Peter Edwards
Francis Levett	Thomas Forbes
Jacobus Kip	John Leslie
Robert Scott	John Mowbray
William Moss	Benjamin Lord
William McLeod	Robert Baillie

---

[37] Identified by other authors as a Major General in the British army.

References Cited

Coker, William S. and Thomas D. Watson
1986. Indian traders of the southeastern Spanish borderlands: Panton, Leslie & Company and John Forbes & Company, 1783-1847. University of West Florida Press; Pensacola Florida.

Griffin, Patricia C.

1983. Chapter Five. The Spanish Return: The People-Mix Period. 1784 - 1821. In The Oldest City, St. Augustine Saga of Survival, Jean Parker Waterbury, editor. St. Augustine Historical Society, St. Augustine Florida.

1990. Mullet on the Beach, The Minorcans of Florida, 1768-1788. El Escribano, The St. Augustine Journal of History, Volume 27. The St. Augustine Historical Society, Florida.

Hill, Roscoe
1916. Descriptive Catalogue of the Documents Relating to the History of the United States in the Papeles Procedentes de Cuba Deposited in the Archivo General de Indias at Seville. Washington, D.C.; Carnegie Institution of Washington.

Lockey, Joseph Byrne
1949. East Florida, 1783-1785. Berkeley; University of California Press.

Mills, Donna Rachel
1992. Florida's First Families: Translated Abstracts of pre-1821 Spanish Censuses. Mills historical press; Tuscaloosa Alabama and Naples Florida.

Mowat, Charles Loch
    1964. East Florida as a British Province, 1763-1784. University of Florida Press; Gainesville.

Quinn, Jane
    1975. Minorcans in Florida, Their History and Heritage. Mission Press, St. Augustine Florida.

Rasico, Philip D.
    1990. The Minorcans of Florida: Their History, Language and Culture. Luthers; New Smyrna Beach.

Schafer, Daniel L.
    1983. Chapter Four, "...not so gay a Town in America as this..." 1763 - 1784. In The Oldest City, St. Augustine Saga of Survival, Jean Parker Waterbury, editor. St. Augustine Historical Society; St. Augustine Florida.

Tanner, Helen Hornbeck
    1989. Zespedes in East Florida, 1784-1790. University of North Florida Press; Jacksonville, Florida.

Index of Personal Names

Acosta Guadarrama, Mateo 88
Alcantara, Antonio 48
Alexander, Henry 89
Allen, Thomas 33
Amoss, Adan 10
Anderson, Tomas 40
Andres, Juan 23
Andreu, Antonio 48
Andreu, Juan 87
Andreu, Thomas 24
Andrews, Samuel 66
Ansel, Martin 5
Ansiau, Francisco 16
Anthrobus, Juan 41
Apunién, Antonio 17
Armstrong, Fleetwood 30, 86
Arnau, Bernardo 46
Arnau, Joseph 19
Arons, Jorje 79
Arredondo, Don Fernando 89
Ashbraner, Felipe 68
Ashley, Nathaniel 61
Ashley, William 81
Ashton, Eduardo 38
Ashworth. *See* Josef Ashworth
Ashworth, Arturo 68
Ashworth, Josef 4, 70
Austin, David 69
Auston. *See* David Austin
Backhayse. *See* Backhouse
Backhouse, Jorje 39
Badell, Pedro 20
Baer, Jacobo 58
Bagley, Josiah 52
Bagueri, Ansel 19

Bailie, Alexandro 71
Bailie, Juan 57, 61
Baillie, Robert 90
Baillon, Ysaac 24
Bailye 66. *See also* Juan Bailie
Baker, Jacobo 55
Ball, Colonel Don Elias 47, 83
Bann, Jacobo 57
Bannes 65
Barnes, Jorge (*or* Jorje) 27, 28, 86
Barnit, Jacobo 45
Barrow, Thomas 54
Barti, Antonio 46
Barton, Enoc 53
Batingoy, Jacobo 5
Bausina, Bartholome 22
Bean, Juan 7
Bedell, Pedro 87
Bee, Thomas 87
Begbie, Alexandro 30
Beggby, Guillermo 37
Bell 61, 62
Beney, Alexandro 53
Bennix, Thomas 60
Berbe, Juan 46
Berry, Michael 81
Bila. *See* Francisco Vila
Bishop, Elijah 81
Bishop, William 81
Bivins, Francisco 57
Black, David 24
Black, Jacob 29
Blackman, Wood 78
Blackwell, Esteban 65
Blunt, Redden 65
Blyk, Juan 2

Boak, Don Thomas 10, 86
Bodd, widow 89.
   See also Henry Alexander
Bogian (or Bogin), Guillermo 73
Boland, Juan 44
Bollison, Francisco 4
Bolton, Robert 81
Bona, Guillermo 40
Boneli (or Bonelly), Jose 50
Borgo, Francisco de 88
Borjeis or Borseis.
   See Thomas Burgess
Bouden, Ysac 69
Boyes (or Boyce), Isabel 41
Brackstone, Guillermo 74
Bradley, Josef 72
Braker (or Brakor), Joraje 73
Brandon, Samuel 58
Bremarach, Pedro 15
Briant, Langley 2, 4, 12, 69
Briart. See Langley Briant
Brid, Juan 86
Briton, Francisco 59
Broddy, Juan 35
Bron. See William Brown
Brown, Captain 26
Brown, Carlos 44
Brown, Colonel 14, 26, 88
Brown, Don Guillermo.
   See William Brown
Brown, Gualtero 3
Brown, Hugo 72
Brown, Juan 67
Brown, Pedro 62
Brown, William 13
Bruce, Simon 58
Bruciantiny 15

Bryant, Hawkins 81
Buchani, Jose 49
Buchantine, Luis 15
Buchentiny.
   See Luis Buchantine
Buchoni. See Jose Buchani
Buckingham, Clias 75
Buderfort, Jacobo 28
Bunkley, Britain 76
Burchani (or Burcham), Josef 2
Burgess, Thomas 35, 56, 86
Burnett, Juan 7
Burns, Jacobo 31
Burton, Ana 44
Butler, Captain 3
Bynum, Jacobo 79, 86
Cabler, Adan 66
Cade 59. See also Juan Cade
Cade, Juan 36
Cala, Pedro de 88
Caldas, Pedro de 22
Cameron, Ana 26
Cameron, Donaldo 39, 65
Campbee, Juan. See Campbell
Campbell, John 73
Camps, Don Pedro 15
Candioli, Francisco 24
Cann, Mr. 72
Cañon, Rusero 28
Canovas, Antonio 49
Canoves. See Antonio Canovas
Capelde, Luis 47
Capella, Lorenzo 19
Capo, Juan 23
Capo, Lorenzo 14
Caravach, Jose 46
Cardona, Jose Hernandez 18

Cargan, Daniel 72
Carguel, Dona Ororia 42
Carmichael, Jacobo 57
Carney, Arturo 86
Carrera. See Juan Carreras
Carreras (or Carreres), Jose 24
Carreras (or Carreres), Juan 19
Carter, Thomas 61
Casals, Vicente 48
Castlake, Samuel 74
Cavedo, Ines 17
Cavedo, Juan, the Younger 17
Cesar [black slave] 89
Chanela, Jose 26
Chanopli. See Juan Granopoli
Chanopoly. See Juan Granopoli
Chapel, Jacobo 80
Chapman, Guillermo 73, 86
Chemares, Rafael 23
Chenoble, Ana Maria 33
Cheny, Beley 86
Chonopla, Juan 46
Christie, Maria 41, 86
Chuaneda, Jose 17
Chuariedas, Juan 18
Claguer 45
Clak. See Jorje Clav
Clar. See Jorje Clav
Clarke 5, 33
Clarke, Dona Honoria 13, 86
Clarke, Jacobo 32
Clarke, Juan 57
Clarke, Thomas 59, 78
Clarke, Tomas 2
Clarkson, Maria 37
Clasworthy, Jacobo 77
Clav, Jorje 19

Clements, James 65
Clemmons, James 65
Close, Juan 43
cobe. See Micajah Coue
Cobham, Don Thomas 51
Coin, Benjamin 41
Colbert, Jacobo 54
Cole, Juana 77
Coll, Sebastian 47
Colliday, Jacob 68
Collins, David 60
Collins, Guillermo 86
Collins, Tompsy 57
Colman, Ricardo 7
Colomines. See Columinas
Columinas, Juan 46
Comebest, Simon 79
Conway Ladson 6
Conway, Carlos 76
Conway, Guillermo 77
Cook, Isabel 26, 36
Cooper, Isabel 42
Corbert, Mr. 71
Corbett, Don Eduardo 51
Cordery, Thomas 35
Cornic, Jose 28
Cornwallis, Count 87
Cosifacho, Pedro 16
Costa, Miguel 60
Coue, Micajah 66
Coulson, Thomas 4
cove. See Micajah Coue
Cox, Carlos 41
Cox, Thomas 33
Cozifaccy, Pietro. See Cosifacho
Crafford. See Juan Crawford
Crane, Spencer 43

Crawford, Juan 73
Crawford, Thomas 37
Cressel, Jorge 31
Crier, Morgan 79
Crosbie, Juan 55
Cruden, Don Juan 52
Crudi, Hermano 78
Crum, Solomon 63
Cuitt, Amos 66
Cunningham, Alexandro 31
Cunningham, Guillermo 1
Cupsted, Juan 41
Curtis, Benjamin 33
Curtis, Guillermo 31, 35, 60, 86
Cuthbert, Jacobo 36, 86
Dabes, vacant ranch of 75
Dampier, Estevan 65
David. See Andres Deveu
David, Guillermo 86
Davidson, Alexandro 45
Davis, Guillermo 6
Davis, Thomas 66
Deewalt, Daniel 27
Delegall, Sara 30, 86
Dell, Phelip 79, 86
Denny ("poor Englishman") 88
Denny, Samuel 74
Depuy, Isac 27
Derry, Mr. 70
Devaux, Diego 89
Deveaux, Jacob 89
Devert. See Andres Deveu
Deveu, Andres 35
DeWaldt, Pedro 40
Dickson, Aron 39
Dobleow, Juan 30
Doemis, Carlos 26

Doharty, Jacobo 66
Doran, Juan 60
Dort, Guillermo 43
Douglas, Colonel 57
Douglas, Don Juan 52
Douglas, Maria 77
Douglass. See Don Juan Douglas
Downer, Moises 68
Drayton, Lu 89
Drennen, David 67
Drew, William 81
Drury, Mills 63
Du Vaux, Colonel 88
Duget, Don Guillermo 12
Duncan, Guillermo 39
Dupuy, Isac 42
Ebner, Jacob 81
Edwards, Don Pedro 10
Edwards, Peter 90
Egan, Stephen 8, 79, 90
Egger, Juan 80, 86
Egmont, Earl of 8
Eleonor, Thomas 39
Eliot, Carlos 87
Elleby, Ysham 76
Elsberry Peters, Solomon 68, 86
Elsini, Antonio 21
English, Juan 42, 43
English, Roberto 25
Esom, Juan 63
Espinosa, Jose 23
Estafanofa, Jorge 48
Estefanople, Jorje 46
Estefanople, Nicolas 17
Esteve, Sebastian 15
Etienne, Sebastian 15
Evans, Mary 18

Evans, Margarita 58
Evans, Thomas 59
Evelin, Juan 44
Evinger, Gotlieb 64
Ewing, Guillermo 57
Fagan, Jacobo 35
Falani, Ferdinando 50
Falconer, Juan 12
Farguson, Juan 8
Farley, Don Samuel 13
Fatany, Ferdinando 50
Fatil 60
Fatio, Don Francisco Felipe 3, 7
   8, 50, 64, 89
Felts, Susana 77
Fenner, Jose 8
Fergtet, Adam 3
Ferre (*or* Ferrer *or* Ferri), Juan
   45, 46
Ferrio, French overseer 71
Ferrio, Jose 49, 71
Fezua. *See* Pedro Flusia
Fich, Juan 59
Fich, Mister 47
Fiche, Master 38, 39
Ficher, Juan 37, 86
Figuera, Bartolome 20
Files, Estevan 72
Fincher, Jesse 63
Fish, Don Jese. *See* Jesse Fish
Fish, Don Jesse 15, 17, 47, 53
Fitch, Andrews 81
Flake, Juan 70
Flanagan Arnuro, Juan 65
Flanagan, Juan 27, 32, 35, 60
Flanagan, Miguel 32
Fleming, Thomas 57

Flemming, Don Jorje 10, 86
Fletcher, Josiah 78
Fleuret, Francisco 73
Flix, Master 37
Flood, Michael 51
Flusia, Pedro 50
Fluxa (*or* Fluixa), Juan 21
Fluxa (*or* Fluixa), Pedro 23
Flyming Oneal 10
Foche, Luis 17
Forbes, Dona Dorotea 53
Forbes, Jacobo 5
Forbes, Thomas 90
Forester, Alexandro 72
Forrester, Juan 54
Fort, Drury 81
Fowis, Juan 25
Fowler, Jacobo 30
Fox, Benjamin 28
Fox, Juan 31
Francois, Juan 50
Frau, Gabriel 50
Freemantle, Samuel 38
Fregin, Jorje 78
French, Robert 81
Friday. *See* David Fridig
Fridig, David. 75
Frost, Jesse 55
Fuerson, Samuel 34
Gale, Senor 52
Garmaldo, Eulalia 48
Garret, Don Joshuah 54
Gerald, Mr. 88
Gibson, Gideon 70
Gilbert. *See* Roberto Guilbert
Girimalde, Eulalia 19
Godfrey, Guillermo 62

Goldsby, Thomas 81
Gomila, Jose 49, 86
Gonzales, Juan 50
Goodbread, Philip 81
Gordon, Adan 54
Gordon, Jacobo 54
Gracias. *See* Miguel Grasias
Gracies. *See* Miguel Grasias
Graham 3, 52. *See also* Grant
Granopoli, Juan 15
Grant, Colonel James 3, 52, 90
Grasias, Miguel 18
Grassel 42, 43
Gray, Archibaldo 71, 86
Gray, Juan 88
Gray, Samuel 81
Graystock, Mr. 6
Grazies. *See* Miguel Grasias
Green, Guillermo 42
Grenier, Nicolas 61
Griffith, Cornelio 80
Grigly, Ricardo 26
Gueli, Guillermo 13
Guilbert, Roberto 69
Guillermo, Juan 71
Guna, Captain 88
Guy, Jacobo 41
Halberto, Juan 37
Hall, Carlos 4
Hall, Juan 69, 70
Hall, Nathaniel 81
Hallen. *See* Thomas Allen
Hallums, Sara 77
Hambly, Juan 3
Hanagan. *See* Juan Flanagan
Harleston, Edward 87
Harnau. *See* Bernardo Arnau

Harris, Guillermo 69
Harrison (brother of Samuel) 6
Harrison, Juan 38
Harrison, Samuel 6
Hawke, Lord 3
Hechol, Maria 49
Hector (black slave) 89
Hedges, Captain John 90
Heineman, Barbara 86
Heley, Don Juan 13, 86
Hely 43, 56. *See also* Heley
Hemdricks, Juan 78
Henar, Esteban 34
Henat. *See* Henar, Esteban
Henderson 25
Henderson, Barbara 83
Henderson, Susana 36
Hendrick, Guillermo 63
Henis, Juan 72
Hephensan, Jorje 60
Hermans, Pedro 66
Hernandez Victor 19
Hernandez Victori 19
Hernandez, Diego 18
Hernandez, Martin 47
Hernandez, Matheo 49
Hewitt, Sara 41
Hobard, Carlos 52
Hodge, David 7, 41
Hohlinan. *See* Jose Holman
Holaway, Samuel 70
Holland, Juan 33, 40, 44, 59
Hollingirth. *See* Hollinsworth
Hollinsworth, Timoteo 33
Holman, Jose 64
Holmes, Don Juan 13
Hombard, Bernardo 31, 38, 86

Honbart. *See* Hombard
Hope, Don Roberto 54
Hopkins, lives in house of 5, 38
Hopkins, Juan (ship master) 74
Hopkins, Juan (shoemaker) 44
Hopton, Abner. 75
Hor, Ponsi 36
Houston, Juan 7
How, Nathaniel 79
Howard, Abrahan 68
Howard, Don Carlos 39, 89
Hudson, Don Juan 18-19
Hudson, Juan 30
Hughes, Jacobo 58
Hughes, Jose 8
Hulint, Thomas 70
Humbard. *See* Hombard
Hume, Don Jacobo 14
Humphrys, David 7
Humphrys, Jacobo 60
Humphrys, Juan 7
Hungerpeler, Jacobo. 75
Hunter, Roberto 78
Hutson, Rush 81
Huwe. *See* Jacobo Hughes
Hyde, Godfredo 56
Imrie. *See* Imry, Juan
Imry, Juan 27
Ingram, Guillermo 76
James, John 87
Jenkins, Richard 81
Jmant, Juan 83
Jo, Negro 87
Johnson (the tavern keeper) 44
Johnson, Don Juan 13, 86
Johnson, Guillermo 28, 86
Johnson, Jorge 76

Johnson, Juan 38
Johnson, Maria 56
Johnston, Guillermo 66
Johnston, Juan 75
Jones, Guillermo 42
Jones, Jacob 62
Jones, Ricardo. 56
Jones, Thomas 29
Junno, Mr. 45
Jusovat, Juan 17
Kane, Guillermo 7
Kane, William 88
Karrel, Jacobo 80, 86
Kean. *See* Guillermo Kane
Keary. *See* Jesse Leary
Keller, Gaspar 76
Keller, Juan 67
Keller, Juana 58
Kelly, Jose 25
Kemp, George 90
Kenesbach, Ysabel 43
Kennedy, August *or* Auguje 58
Ker. *See* Jorje Kerr
Kerr, Alan 24
Kerr, Jorje 28
Kertlan, Guillermo 38
King, Ricardo 74
King, Robin 2
King, Sebastian 67
King, Solomon 81
Kip, Jacobus 90
Klepter, Juan 55
Ladson, Juan 6
Laird, Jacobo 8
Lambert, Jacobo 4
Lane, Guillermo 61
Lane, Pearce 61

Lapin, Maria 58
Laun, Don Carlos 37
Laws, Juan 86
Leary, Jesse 77
Ledford, Federico 69
Ledo, Antonio 55
Legge, Eduardo 63
Leonardi, Roque 14, 28
Leonardy. See Roque Leonardi
Leonor, Roque. See Leonardi
Lermont, Roberto 43
Leslie, Don Juan or John 53, 90
Leslie, Josef 42
Lessam. See Roberto Letson
Letson, Roberto 44
Levett. See Don Francisco Levit
Levett, Francis. See Levit
Levit, Don Francisco 53, 57, 90
Lewis, Jacobo 42
Linder, Juan [Senior] 1
Linder, Juan [Junior] 71
Linham, Guillermo 86
Linsay, Page 4
Llafrui. See Bartolome Lloufri
Llambias, Antonio 51
Llambies. See Antonio Llambias
Llopis, Bartholome 24
Lloufri, Bartolome 21
Lofton, Juan 61
Lopis. See Bartolome Llopis
Lord, Benjamin 34, 90
Lorenza, Paula 20
Lorenzo, Juan 48
Lorimer, Alexandro 29
Love, Juan 40, 86
Lovett. See Levit, Francisco
Lowry, Luis 68

Lowther, Jacobo 30
Lucas, William 81
Lufton, Juan 61
Lysett, Patricio. 75
Mabrionat, Anastario 20
Mabromaty. See Mabrionat
Macan, Hubo 39
MacArthur, General Archibald iv, 59, 88
MacArthur, Juan 55, 56
Macboy, Juan 45, 55
MacClearan, Guillermo 33
MacCormick, Jose 72
MacCullch, Tomathon 69
MacCuller, Jonatan 55
MacCuller, Josef 55
MacDaniel, Guillermo 55
MacDermott, Juan 74
Macdon, Isabel 5
MacDonal, Jacobo 30
Macdonal, Lucrecia 58
MacDonald, Reynaldo 74
Macdonald, Alexandro 70
Macdonald, Patricio 55
MacDonell, Alexandro 74
MacDonell, Randolfo 74
MacFarlan, Juan 40, 86
Macfarland, Juan 44
MacGirit, Daniel 3, 72
MacGirit, Jacobo 71
MacGirt , Jayme. See MacGirit
Macguin, Neal 29
MacHenry, Guillermo 15, 51
Machogui, Joaquin 17
MacIntosh, William. See MacYntosh, Don Guillermo
MacKenzie, Don Juan 11

Mackenzie, Daniel 41
MacKinnon, Don Guillermo 11
MacLatchy, Carlos 53, 54
Maclenan (apprentice boy) 40
MacLeod, Donald 77
Macleod, Jacobo 66
Macleod, Rodrigo 36
Macoy, Jacobo 77
Macpheal, Margarita 36
Macphearson, Duncan 45
Macquin, Alexandro 36
Macragh, Felipe 40
Macreddy, David 12
Maculler, Joseph.
   See MacCuller
MacYntosh, Don Guillermo 54
Maestre, Pedro 50
Makoy, Juan 14
Maliard, Daniel 70
Mall, Thomas 69
Manen, Eduardo 38
Mangum, Guillermo 1
Mangun.
   See Mangum, Guillermo
Manus, Nazaniel 42
Manwel, Thomas 55
Marchal, Manuel 24
Marcos, Andres 17
Marin, Francisco 18
Marran, Lady 39
Marran, David 25, 57
Marrant. *See* David Marran
Marshall, Juan 28, 33
Martin, Alexandro 45
Martin, Don Juan 9, 17
Martin, John 90
Martin, Mathews 70

Martineli, Domingo 16
Marzail. *See* Manuel Marchal
Mason, Ysabel 26
Masux, Christobal 31
Mauromati. *See* Mabrionat
Maxwell, Gullermo 27
Mayfield, Estevan 62, 72
McGirt. *See* Jacobo MacGirit
McGirth. *See* Daniel MacGirit
McKenzie. *See* Juan MacKenzie
McLeod, William 90
Medici, Elias 16
Megy, Francisco 24
Mercer, Juan 30
Merlin, Eduardo 83
Mestre, Antonio 50
Meter, Don Guillermo 83
Meyes, Juana Maria 16
Meyrhaven, Margarita 41
Michel, Juan 13
Michi, Carlos 30
Micky, Juan 58
Miguins, Juan 42
Millegan. *See* Sara Mullegan
Miller, Ricardo 67
Mills, Josef 69
Mills, Theofilo 55
Milor, Carlos 27
Milton, Miguel 62
Mir, Antonio 46
Mitchell, Guillermo 73
Mitchell, Juan 37
Mofet, Roberto 27
Moises, David 25, 37, 86
Monerief, Colonel 44
Montel, Antonio 36
Moor, Francisco 40

Moor, Jacobo 86
Moor, Juan 40
Moor, Samuel 88
Moore, Philip 90
Moore, Thomas 83
More, Jacobo 64
More 44,
More, Dorotea 36, 86
More, Hanah 64
More, Mistress 58
More, Thomas 35
Moris, Juan. See Morris
Morpus, Riccardo 66
Morris, Don Juan 13, 52
Mortimer, Eduardo 13
Moses 25
Moss, Don Jacobo 12
Moss, William 90
Mott, Hanah 4
Motte, Jacobo 58
Moultrie, Lieutenant Governor John 90
Mountrie, Austin 60
Mowbray, Don Juan (John) 44, 83, 90
Muffett 27
Muhie, Carlos 83
Mulkey, Juan. 76
Mullegan, Sara 56
Murphy, Guillermo 3
Murphy, Juan 73
Murphy, Thomas 70
Murray, Don Ricardo Donaban 53
NAME MISSING 2, 3, 5, 65
Naper, Juan 56
Napoles, Antonio Estevan 16

Neal, Thomas 68
Neeley, Christobal 2, 60
Neeley, Major 80
Neeley, Roberto 2
Neely, Cristobal. See Neeley, Christobal
Negra, Maria 88
Negra, Mary or Maria 87
Negro Pedro 88
Negro Primus 88
Negro, Carlos 89
Negro, Cyrus or Cyro 88
Negro, Ham 87
Negro, Joe 88
Negro, John 88
Negro, Katy 88
Negro, Robin 87
Negro, Sandy 87
Negro, Saunders 87
Negro, Sharper 88
Newberry, Enrique 29, 35, 86
Newell, Ana 43
Nix, Eduardo 30
Noland, Jacobo 67
Noris, Juan 51
O'Neil. See Enrique Onell
Oaets, Tamer 73
Oates, Guillermo 59
Obrien, Luis 45
Ogilvie, Major Francis 90
Ohuli, Jacobo 42
OLeary, Derby 25, 34
Oneill, Don Jacobo 10
Onell, Don Enrique 80
Onell, Enrique 61
Oria, Arturo 6
Orr, Don Thomas 10, 36, 86

Ortega, Ignacio 23
Ortegas, Ignacio.
    See Ignacio Ortega
Ortega, Lazaro 20
Ortegas, Lazaro.
    See Lazaro Ortega
Ortega, Sebastian 16
Ortega, Sebastian the Younger 16
Ortegas, Sebastian.
    See Sebastian Ortega
Pace, David. 76
Pace, Willis 6
Pacetti. See Andres Pachete
Pachete, Andres 20
Paiyne, Enrique. 44
Palmer, Martin 4
Panton 3, 36, 53, 64
Panton and Leslie. See Panton
Panton, House of. See Panton
Pantor 58. See also ? Panton
Parr, Tomas 64
Paseo, Pedro 48
Pasety. See Andres Pachete
Pastel, Mr. 88
Paterson, Alexandro 28, 57
Patrick, Daniel and Samuel 63
Pau, Antonio 55
Pau, Jacinto 32
Payne, Robert 90
Pazeti. See Andres Pachete
Peavett. See Don Jose Pevit
Peavett, Mary Evans 18
Pedman, Mr. 49
Pedro de Bordo, Pepe 45
Pedro de Burgo, Pepino.
    See Pepe Pedro de Bordo

Pedro, Guillermo 86
Pedro, Thomas 86
Pedulach, Demetrio 21
Pehgrin, Matheo 21
Peirgler, Enrrique 77
Pelegrin. See Matheo Pehgrin
Pelegrin, Bartolome 45
Pellicer. See Francisco Pelliser
Pelliser, Francisco 16
Pengree, Guillermo 73, 75
Penticost, Hartivel 81
Perpal, Mistress.
    See Perpal, Ysabal
Perpal, Ysabel 32, 37, 47, 58
Perpat. See Perpal, Ysabal
Pesso di Borgo, Francesco.
    See Pepe Pedro de Bordo
Peters, Solomon 80, 86
Pevit, Don Jose 7, 11, 12
Philips, Jorje 71
Phillips, Daniel 67
Phillips, Juan 67
Piles, Juan 36
Piles, Sara 37
Plummer, Daniel 62
Pobey, Ricardo 38
Pons, Jacobo 44
Pons, Jose 20, 28, 47, 86, 88
Pons, Mathias 22
Pool, Ricardo 29
Pope, Gaspar 20
Popee. See Gaspar Pope
Popi. See Gaspar Pope
Portell, Juan 21
Portella. See Juan Portell
Porter, Rosa 37
Powell, Guillermo 80

Powell, Jorfe Henderson 86
Poyner, Josef 76
Pozo de Borgo, Francisco.
  See Pepe Pedro de Bordo
Prais. See Jaime de Prat
Prat, Jaime de 24
Prats. See Jaime de Prat
Prescot, Felse 81
Pritchard, Eduardo 6
Pritchard, Roberto 63
Proctor, Mrs. 5
Proctor, Edward 81
Proctor, Felipe 72
Puselograpo, Francisco 22
Pyne, Diego 51
Quenaud, Juan Pedro 77
Quni, Bernardo 36
Rain, Jose 62
Rech, Maestre 51
Reddy, Guillermo 68
Reed, Roberto 45, 86
Rees, Guillermo 59
Rein (Black slave) 89
Reina (Black slave) 89
Reynolds, Juan 11, 26, 86
Riccio the Italian 33
Ridabert, Ylisbet 49
Rigby, Thomas 30, 86
Robertson, Enrique 26, 38
Robins, Josef 86
Robinson, Don Jose 9
Robinson, Francisco 43
Robinson, Juan 38
Robinson, Juana 43
Roger, Roberto 47
Rogers, Gaspar 63
Rogue, Don Santiago de la 9

Roke, Samuel 68
Rolles. See Don Dionis Rolles
Rolles, Don Dionis 64, 65, 71
Rollins, Benjamin 4
Rollison, Francisco 4
Rols, Juan 8
Rose, Jose 21
Ross, Josef. See Jose Rose
Ross, John 90
Ross, Malcolmó 33, 44
Ross, Malcomo.
  See Malcolmó Ross
Ross, Thomas 90
Russel, Guillermo 62
Ryan, Juan 59
Sabater, Pablo 47
Sabatier. See Pablo Sabater
Safold, Ysham 71, 86
Sala, Nicolas 51
Salada. See Nicolas Sala
Salata. See Nicolas Sala
Sally, Enrique 67
Salord, Francesc.
  See Salort, Francisco
Salort, Francisco 23
Sam (Black slave) 89
Sampson, Juan 59
Samson. See Jacobo Samson
Samson, Jacobo 29, 60
Sanches, Francisco. See Sanchez
Sanchez, Francisco 15, 71
Sanfort, Jacobo 6
Sanson, Jacobo.
  See Jacobo Samson
Sante, Pasqual de 23
Scat, Don Juan 60.
  See also Don Roberto Scott

See also Don Roberto Scott
Scotland, Jacobo 25, 57, 86
Scott, Don Roberto 14, 60, 90
Scott, John 81
Segui, Bernardo 22
Segui, Juan 22
Segui, Miguel 16
Selom. *See* Juan Solom
Selord.
    See Salort, Francisco
Sheriff, Don Pedro 12, 86
Shever, Judith 40
Shireman, Felipe 76
Shirreff. *See* Don Pedro Sheriff
Shocker, Gaspar 68
Shoemaker, Daniel 80, 86
Siblet, William 81
Sigui, Diego 22
Simpson, Guillermo 64, 86
Simpson, Thomas 30, 86
Sims, Guillermo 33
Sims, Roberto 59
Sisley, Martin 81
Slater, Guillermo 34, 86
Sloan, Jacobo 76
Smart, Ysac 41
Smith, (widow) Ana 40, 41
Smith, Benjamin 72
Smith, Carlos 69
Smith, Enrique 74
Smith, Ezekiel 81
Smith, Guillermo 70
Smith, Jacobo 26, 75
Smith, Levis 62
Smith, Roberto 60
Smylie, Juan 64
Snell, Enrique 75

Soche, Luis 19
Solano, Manuel 48
Solom, Antonio 21
Solom, Juan 17
Spalding, Don Jacobo 11
Spalding, Ysham 77
Spence, Don Roberto 52
Spicer, Christopher 69, 86
Spindler, Sebastian 59
Splaun, Guillermo 78
Stafford, Roberto 70
Stafford, Thomas 3
Stage, Federico 35, 86
Steed, Thomas 44
Stefanopoly, Antonio 51
Steigler, Juan 78
Stephason, Diego 80
Sterling, Francisco 73
Steward, Captain Don Juan 54
Stewart, late Colonel 11
Stewart, Matheo 26
Stoop, Pedro 47
Stopa. *See* Pedro Stoop
Storr, Don Juan 12, 86
Stoughtenmire, Jorje 75
Stout, Jose 6
Strong, Guillermo 56
Stuard, Antonio 57
Stubbs, Wade 70
Suitas, Madalena 17
Sullivan, Daniel 78
Summerlin, Peter 81
Sutherland, John 2
Sutton, Beaman 61
Swanson, David 79
Swiney, Enrique 61
Swiney, Maria 6

Syks, Margarita 57
Tailor, Ysabel 43
Tallack, Jorje 78
Tallani, Francisco 21
Tanning, Master.
 See Juan Tannyng
Tannyng, Juan 4, 43
Tarberry 87
Tate, Jeremiah 81
Tate, William 81
Taylor, David 42
Taylor, Isabel 44, 56
Taylor, Jacobo 28, 86
Taylor, Jose 56
Taylor, Roberto 62
Tedulache.
 See Demetrio Pedulach
Tenencys, Pedro 61
Tennant, Juan 31
Terbert, Jose 29
Theo, Antonio 46
Thomas, Juan 32
Thompson 6
Thompson, Thomas 43
Thorp, Allen 78
Tompson, Jorje 86
Tomson, Jacobo 65
Tonin. See Tonyn, Patrick
Tonyn. See Tonyn, Patrick
Tonyn, Field Marshal.
 See Tonyn, Patrick
Tonyn, Patrick 15, 31, 40, 43,
 49, 69, 85, 90
Touchstone, Esteban 68, 86
Towin, Roberto 7
Travies. See Aaron Travis
Travis, Aaron 71

Tremol, Francisco 19
Trian, Juan 46
Triay, Gabriel 48
Triay, Juan 22, 46
Triay, Pedro 21
Trope, Pedro 50
Truchet, Carlos 63
Tuday, Daniel 86
Tudy, Jacobo 41
Tuffts, Simon 25
Tuhis, Simon. See Simon Tuffts
Tumio, Don Tomas 11
Tunno. See Tumio, Don Tomas
Turnbull, house rented from 45
Turnbull, David 36, 37
Turnbull, Michel 9
Tustin, Tomas 70
Tweed, Catalina 26
Tweedy, Thomas 31, 36
Vas, Loclin. See Vass Lachlam
Vass, Major Lachlam 2, 52
Vchuaart, Don Alexander 87
Vedell 87
Vila, Francisco 48
Villalonga, Antonia 49
Villalonga, Juan 48
Villalonga, Miguel 23
Villaronga, Ambros 49
Vish, Jorje 33, 34
Waldron, Luisa 5
Wales, Jacobo 42, 86
Wallace, Captain 87
Wallace, Jacobo 31
Wansey, Davins 34
Warantine, Guillermo 65
Ward 64
Ward, Juan 65

Ward, Juana 24, 39
Ware, Juan 60
Warington, Nicolas 26, 35
Warner, Josiah 59
Warner, Pedro 67
Warner, Ysabel 83
Warrington.
   See Nicolas Warington
Waters, Sinclair 34
Waters, Thomas 32
Watkins, Juan 30, 39
Watson 49
Wauer, Jose 39.
   See also Weaver
Weaver, John 37
Weaver, Josef 38.
   See also Wauer
Welsh, Mrs. 5
Welsh, Nicolas 63
Werin, Juan 87
Westley, Jacobo 66
Whaley, Guillermo 72
Whaly, Juan 79
White, Enrique 64
White, Estevan 67
White, Jacobo 5, 62
Whiteman, Jacobo 67
Whitman, Guillermo 75
Whitmore, Roberto 65, 86
Wigengs. *See* Jose Wiggins
Wiggins, Jose 64
Wilkinson, Mr. 70
Williams, Enrique 7
Williams, Evan 56

Williams, Juan 80, 86
Williams, Major 89
Williams, Samuel 71
Williams, William 81
Williams, Wilson 65
Wilson, Samuel 61
Wimbesley, Abraham 79
Wise, Juan 76
Woltz, Gaspar 64
Wood, Don Juan 9
Wordin, Thomas 74
Wornal, Miguel 79
Wright, Thomas 86
Wuish. *See* Jorje Vish
Ximenes. *See* Rafael Chemares
Yabes, Lorenzo 28
Yallowley.
   See Joshua Yarrowley
Yanes, Lorenzo 42, 50
Yarrowley, Joshua 56
Yeates, Don David 52
Yeats. *See* Don David Yeates
Yesefes, Don 31
Yewbank, Estevan 80, 86
Young, Alexandro 2, 12, 86
Young, Don Guillermo 54, 58, 64, 80
Young, Juan 79, 86
Young, Samuel 79, 86
Young, Thomas 59
Youngblood, Jese 79, 86
Yuercon, Mr. 57
Zubly, David 39

Index of Origins

Alsace France 38, 79
Alayor Minorca 16, 21, 23, 24, 46, 48, 49
America 2, 58, 73
Andalucia, Spain 22
Bahamas 34
Barcelona, Spain 46
Basel, Switzerland 1
Bermuda 5
Berne, Switzerland 8
Boston, Massachusetts 25, 33, 60
Brest, France 58
Carolina 71
Charleston, South Carolina 27, 32
Ciudadela, Minorca 16, 19, 20, 22, 23, 46, 47, 48
Corsica 15, 16, 17, 22, 45, 46, 48, 51
Crete, Greece 21
[East] Florida 15, 48. *See also* Matanzas and San Augustine
East Indies 39
England 3, 8, 10-14, 26, 27, 29, 30, 32-44, 55-61, 63-68, 69, 70, 72, 74-77, 79
Florence, Italy 21, 50
France 15, 34, 49, 60. *See also* Alsace, Brest, Fracia, *and* Gascony
Fracia [France] 50
Gascony, France 9
Geneva, Switzerland 77
Georgia 5-7, 24, 28-31, 33, 41, 52, 54, 64, 66, 67, 69, 73, 75-77
Germany 26, 27, 31, 43, 55, 64, 66, 67, 73, 75-78.
    See also Prussia *and* Saxony
Great Britain 62
Greek Nation 46. *See also* Crete, Milos island *and* Peloponnesus
Havana, Cuba 32
Infantes 47
Ireland 5, 7, 8, 10, 13, 15, 18, 25, 26, 29, 30, 32-38, 40, 43-45, 51, 53, 55-57, 59, 60, 65, 67, 69, 72-75, 77-78, 80
Italian. *See* Italy

Italy 26, 31, 49, 50. *See also* Florence, Leghorn, Modena, Naples, Tuscany *and* Venice
Jersey. *See* [New] Jersey
Leghorn, Italy 50
Louisiana, 2, 3. *See also* New Orleans
Mahon, Minorca 20, 21, 22, 24, 32, 47, 48, 49, 50, 51
Mallorca, Spain 16, 17
Malta 24, 67
Maryland 5, 38, 61, 64, 69, 72, 79
Mercadal, Minorca 14, 24, 48, 87
Milos island, Greece 20
Minorca 14, 16-24, 32, 45-51. *See also* Alayor, Ciudadela, Mahon, Mercadal and San Felipe
Mississippi 60, 76
Modena, Italy 14
Morea. *See* Peloponnesus
Naples, Italy 20, 23
New England 60
[New] Jersey 4, 44
New Orleans 71, 72
New Providence island, Bahamas 34, 59
New York 7, 40, 53, 56, 59, 63, 79
North Carolina 2, 4, 6, 7, 12, 30, 33, 41-43, 54-56, 58, 59, 61, 62, 64-71, 76, 78, 79
Nova Scotia 36, 64
Peloponnesus Greece ("Morea") 15
Pennsylvania 3, 6-8, 24, 27, 31, 35, 37, 39, 40, 54, 57, 58, 60-63, 67, 68, 70, 72, 73, 75-77, 79, 80
Pensacola, West Florida 45, 57, 71
Persia [?] 31
"Peze" [Basel] 1
Philadelphia [Pennsylvania] 58, 68
Poland 25, 56
Portugal 55
Providence Rhode Island 34
Prussia [?] 31

San Augustine, East Florida 36, 49, 50
San Felipe, Minorca 18, 19, 20, 23, 46
Saxony (Germany) 35
Scotland 2-5, 7-13, 24-31, 33-40, 42-45, 51-53, 56-58, 60, 62, 64, 70, 71, 74, 79
Sitges, Spain 51
Smyrna [today Izmir Turkey] 9, 20
South Carolina 2-7, 13, 14, 26, 28, 33, 36, 37, 39-42, 44, 55, 56, 62-64, 67, 68, 70-80
Sweden 7
Switzerland 59. *See also* Basel, Geneva *and* Berne
Tarragona Spain 18
Transylvania "of the Emperor" [today part of Romania] 6
Turkey 53. *See also* Smyrna
Tuscany, Italy 15, 17, 19, 21, 49
United States 68
Venice, Italy 16, 24
Villanueva y Geltrú near Sitges, Spain 51
Virginia 1, 2, 4-8, 30-32, 36, 40, 42, 56, 57, 60-62, 65-72, 74-80
West Florida 71, 72, 75, 76. *See also* Pensacola

Index of Occupations

accountant 57
agent 38, 53
    for the ranch of Josiah Bagley 52
    of Don Dionis Rolles 65
aide de camp of General MacArthur 59
architect 27
auctioneer 25, 28, 34, 39
Bahamas islands iv, 3, 34
baker 20, 22, 31, 35, 38, 42, 43, 50, 65, 75
    master 31
bar, rent of 33
    bartender 5, 25
    sold drinks 37
beer, trader in 15
blacksmith 18, 30, 32, 41, 46, 61, 64, 67, 76, 79
bugler 66
builder
    of a schooner 63
    of boats and canoes 69
    of machines 27
    of wind and water mills 71
businessmen 10, 11, 12, 13, 51, 52. See also merchant
butcher 35, 42, 44, 57
captain
    in the military 3, 26, 54, 87, 88, 89, 90
    of a ship 26, 31, 87
carpenter 2, 3, 5, 6, 7, 15-17, 28, 30, 31, 33, 34, 36, 40-44, 47-49, 51, 56, 63, 65-70, 74, 75, 77-80. See also ship's carpenter
cashier
    for merchant 43
    for seaborne commerce 36
    of business 30
    of commercial house 26
chairmaker 26, 34, 75
chaplain 49

Chief Justice of the English governor 14
clerk 38, 58
Clerk of the Council 52
colonel 9, 11, 26, 54, 55, 57, 80, 87, 88, 90
commissioner
    for Evacuation 13
    for South American sequestered goods 52
cooper 24, 30, 31
cutler 35
customs Head 13
dry goods, seller of 59, 72
day laborer 60, 63, 72
distilled liquor
    and beer, trader in 15
    seller of 19, 25, 45, 59
engineer of the former British government 27
Evacuation, British commissioner for 13
executor of the will of the late colonel Stewart 11
farmer 2-8, 11, 15-25, 27, 28, 32, 35, 38, 39, 41, 42, 45-50, 53, 55-57, 59-80. *See also* planter
firewood keeper 41
fisherman 17-24, 42, 43, 45-47, 50, 58, 68
food, seller of. *See* grocer
foreman 3. *See also* supervisor on the plantation
gardener 5, 15, 31, 39, 77
general iv, 59, 88
glass installer 35, 27
grocer 29, 32, 63
    for dried foods 36, 37, 43
    sells some foods 56
gunsmith 35, 56, 60
herbalist 32
hunter 1
Indian
    Interpreter 4
    trader 2, 3, 12, 64
innkeeper 32

interpreter 12
iron founder 80
joiner 57
laundress 20, 39, 43
lawyer 13, 72
lieutenant 81
lieutenant colonel vi, 9, 90
lieutenant governor 12, 90
linen weaver 46
lives on
    charity 36
    her savings 26, 36, 48
    his savings 35, 36, 59
locksmith 41
major 11, 52, 80, 89, 90
maker
    of carriages 27
    of small boats and canoes 7
    of money 62
mariner. *See* sailor
maritime associated. 51, 79. *See also* sailor, ships *and* navigation
mason 8, 38, 40, 43, 48, 65
master. *See also* ship master
    and owner of a ship 57
    of a schooner 16, 17, 40, 50
    of ship 74
    of ship called the Black Fish 28
    of sloop 17, 44
    of two boats 3
meat chopper 35
member of the lower house of the assembly 11
mercantile 74. *See also* merchant
merchant 25-31, 34, 40, 47, 53, 55, 60, 64. *See also* businessmen
    and trader
navigation, teaching of 51
Notary Head 13
painter 27, 35

physician 9, 14, 32, 51, 59, 60, 73
pilot 19, 26, 28, 45, 59, 78
planter 1-3, 8, 9, 11, 13, 18, 54, 55, 63, 66, 69, 73, 77.
    See also farmer
poultry merchant 37
private secretary of the former governor 10
provincial secretary 52
rope maker 17
saddler 34, 38
sailing master 29, 55, 57
sailor 15, 17, 19, 21, 24, 28, 30, 32, 33, 39, 40, 43, 45, 48-50, 55, 56,
    59, 60, 66, 69, 77
school master 36, 39, 58
seamstress 33, 36, 39, 41, 42, 43, 44, 56
    apprentice 33
sequestered goods, commissioner for South American 52
sergent 72, 79, 81
sexton 14
ships
    associated with 33
    builder 27, 63
    master 51, 57. *See also* master
    carpenter 5, 29, 37, 39, 41-43, 58, 62, 64, 71
shoemaker 4, 5, 18, 21, 25, 30, 35, 37, 44, 55, 64, 73, 74
shopkeeper 16, 22, 36, 37, 45, 48, 67, 72
silversmith 33, 55, 58, 70, 71
soldier 68
steward of the former governor 58
stonecutter 16, 19, 23, 40, 41, 46
store merchant. *See* merchant
sugar refiner 64
supervisor on the plantation 7. *See also* foreman
surgeon 59, 74
surveyor 56
    of the province, former head 34
tailor 5, 17, 26, 31, 33, 34, 35, 38-41, 56, 58, 62, 78
tanner 4, 34, 37, 74.

tavern
    keeper 44
    owner 27
tax
    assessor 76
    collector 13
trader 44, 50, 53, 54. *See also* merchant *and* businessmen
watchmaker 71
weaver 45, 55, 68
wheelwright 68
windlass operator 31
wine trader or merchant 14, 25, 30

Index of Other Subjects

Amalia island, list of residents of 82
Anglican 3
Armory of English 45
assembly, house of the old 54
Black Fish, master of ship called the 28
Carlota street, list of residents of, 82
Catholic vi, 9, 13, 27, 38, 74, 84, 85
canoe 32
"Cedar Point," 69
commerce 28
Creek Indians 12
degenerates 26
dugout canoe 23
El Blof 32
field marshal 40, 43, 49, 69, 85, 90
frigate 32
Greek church 21
Indian affairs 54
Indian boy in household 51
Indian nation 88
Indians 87
Jew vi, 37, 55

Jewish 25
Lutheran 71
Matanzas, East Florida
 fort of 33
 river of 77
Mount Pleasant 7
Mount Tucker ranch 6
Mukoso inlet vii
"Newcastle," locality of 2
New Smyrna, East Florida vii, 68
New Waterford 18
Oak Forest 11
Potberg 73
privates [military rank] 37, 45, 64-66, 72, 73, 81
Protestant 35, 54, 61, 65, 80
Rio del Norte [river of the North] 86
Rio Nasaw [Nasau] 86
River St. John. *See* Rio San Juan
Rio San Juan [St. John river] 2-4, 6, 8, 56, 60, 64-66, 74, 81, 88
 construction of a schooner on 5
San Luis [boat ?] 32
Santa Rosalia [frigate] 33
schooners 6, 12, 16, 56
 used to make trips to the United States 51
 William Maid 14
Seminole Indians 12
shipwreck 32
sloop 32
Talbot island, list of residents of, 82
warehouse for tanners 12, 25.

www.ingramcontent.com/pod-product-compliance
Lightning Source LLC
Chambersburg PA
CBHW072157160426
43197CB00012B/2429